BRIGHT NOTES

DEMIAN
BY
HERMANN HESSE

Intelligent Education

 INFLUENCE PUBLISHERS

Nashville, Tennessee

BRIGHT NOTES: Demian
www.BrightNotes.com

No part of this publication may be used or reproduced in any manner whatsoever without written permission, except in the case of brief quotations in critical articles and reviews. For permissions, contact Influence Publishers http://www.influencepublishers.com.

ISBN: 978-1-645422-10-5 (Paperback)
ISBN: 978-1-645422-11-2 (eBook)

Published in accordance with the U.S. Copyright Office Orphan Works and Mass Digitization report of the register of copyrights, June 2015.

Originally published by Monarch Press.
John Whiton, 1973
2020 Edition published by Influence Publishers.

Interior design by Lapiz Digital Services. Cover Design by Thinkpen Designs.

Printed in the United States of America.

Library of Congress Cataloging-in-Publication Data forthcoming.
Names: Intelligent Education
Title: BRIGHT NOTES: Demian
Subject: STU004000 STUDY AIDS / Book Notes

CONTENTS

1)	Introduction to Hermann Hesse	1
2)	Demian	19
3)	Introduction to Demian	58
4)	Textual Analysis	
	Chapter One: Two Worlds	65
	Chapter Two: Cain	71
	Chapter Three: The Thief Upon The Cross	76
	Chapter Four: Beatrice	80
	Chapter Five: The Bird Struggles Out of The Egg	86
	Chapter Six: Jacob's Struggle	89
	Chapters Seven and Eight: Frau Eva; the Beginning of the End	92
5)	Demian and The Critics	94
6)	Essay Questions and Answers	97
7)	Bibliography	103

HERMANN HESSE

INTRODUCTION

FAMILY BACKGROUND

Like many German writers, Hermann Hesse came from a family which had for many generations been associated with the Protestant clergy. The father, Johannes Hesse, was a protestant clergyman who belonged to the pietistic tradition, a liberal branch of German Protestantism which stressed a concern for the individual's relationship to God above strict formal dogma. Hermann was later to acknowledge the importance of the religious atmosphere of his childhood, as, for example, in a letter dated 1950 in which he spoke of Christianity as it was lived, rather than preached, in his home. Johannes Hesse spent the years 1869 to 1873 as a missionary in India. There he acquired an interest in Oriental philosophy and theology which he was to retain for the rest of his life. Forced to return to Europe on account of poor health, he settled in Calw, a town in Southwestern Germany, where he was active as an author of works on religious subjects. Hermann's mother, Marie, came from a similar background; she had been in India as the wife of a missionary. She was living in Calw after the death of her first husband when she met Johannes Hesse.

Hermann, the second of six children, was born in Calw on July 2nd 1877. Four years later the family moved to Basel, Switzerland, and acquired Swiss citizenship. The father continued his religious work in Basel where he became the editor of a missionary magazine. In 1886 the family returned to Calw where Hesse was to remain until leaving home to attend a boarding school in 1890. Hermann's early childhood years were for the most part pleasant and they were certainly intellectually stimulating. Literature, philosophy, and the arts were discussed and respected in his home. Guests, many of whom came from foreign lands, were often entertained there. Hermann felt an especial affinity to his mother whose loving care provided him with a feeling of security and well-being. His father, on the other hand, in spite of his tolerance in regard to many theological matters, believed in strict discipline and followed rigid theories of education which allowed no room for freedom of expression on his son's part. Many of the difficulties of these early years are reflected in Hesse's works, as, for example, in "A Child's Heart." As a boy, Hermann was not an outstanding pupil and did not enjoy school; he once remarked that he had had only one teacher whom he admired.

SEARCH FOR A CAREER

As was common in Germany at that time, Hermann was sent to a boarding school to prepare for the difficult examination which all students had to pass in order to be admitted to advanced schools and the university. He entered the school in Göppingen in 1890 to undertake this preparation. At this school, for the only time in his life, he was an exceptionally good student. After successfully passing the examination, he followed the wishes of his father and enrolled in the famous school at Maulbronn with the intention of becoming a Protestant minister. The atmosphere of the school soon proved too oppressive and Hermann ran away. He returned, but once more was unable to adjust and soon left the school permanently. The months which followed were exceedingly traumatic for the disturbed youth. Help was sought from various persons and institutions, but Hermann's emotional problems could not be alleviated. Once he even went so far as to attempt suicide. His final exposure to formal education was at a preparatory school in Bad Cannstatt in 1893 and 1894. Hesse was not at all happy there and his experiences formed the basis for the descriptions of some of Sinclair's unhappy school experiences in *Demian*.

While doing mechanical work in a Calw clock factory in 1894 and 1895, the young Hesse decided that he wanted to become a writer. He soon found employment in a bookstore in Tübingen and began to see meaning, or at least potential meaning, in life. In 1899 he published his first books, a collection of poetry and one of short prose pieces. In that same year he moved to Basel where he continued to work in the book trade and to expand his horizons, by reading books of many different kinds, and by traveling in Switzerland and Italy. Two years later he wrote a book which attracted the attention of some important German critics and which accordingly established Hesse's reputation as an author: *The Posthumous Papers and Poems of Hermann Lauscher*.

IMPORTANT EARLY WRITINGS

Other books followed, including, in 1904, the novel *Peter Camenzind*. This book was immediately successful and the royalties from it and from other writings gave Hesse a degree of financial independence. He was accordingly able to leave the book trade and devote himself entirely to his writing. The novel is about a poor but talented Swiss boy who grows up in harmony with nature, but decides to go out into the world where he eventually attains a measure of material success in society. He ultimately comes to realize that he has not found self-fulfillment in love, intellectual pursuits, art, music, or material goods. Following the death of his close friend Boppi, a cripple, he finally retires to lead an isolated life free of the demands of society. Already in the first of Hesse's novels we see very clearly the **theme** that will pervade all of the later ones: the difficult search on the part of an individual for identity and fulfillment.

Hesse soon became a respected member of the German literary elite and contributed stories, poems, reviews, and essays to many of the leading periodicals of that time. He also continued to write novels and the next one, *Beneath the Wheel* (1906), was to a great extent autobiographical. It relates the unsuccessful attempt of the hero, Hans Giebenrath, to cope with the stifling atmosphere of the educational system. The two sides of Hesse's own nature are shown in Hans and in Hermann Heilner, who rebelled against the system and ran away. Hans, like Hesse, experienced many disappointments and eventually found himself unable to cope with the demands of his father and of the school. In two very important respects, however, the novel does not follow Hesse's biography; Hans' mother dies when he is very young, depriving him of a source of warmth and love, and Hans himself, in a state of depression, drowns while still a young man. One of many German literary works of the early twentieth century which attacked the educational system, *Beneath the Wheel* was very popular.

Hesse's next two novels, *Gertrude* (1910) and *Rosshalde* (1914), deal with the problems of the artist. The former is one of the least autobiographical of Hesse's works. The hero, Kuhn, is a musician who enjoyed a happy childhood. He injures his leg in an accident and becomes introverted. He falls in love with Gertrude, but lacks the self-assurance to reveal his feelings to her and try to win her love. She marries another man, but the marriage is not successful and her husband commits suicide. Kuhn becomes a great composer, although he remains a lonely and unhappy person. He has limited contact with Gertrude in his later years, although she continues to be a source of inspiration for his great works of art.

YEARS OF CRISIS

In 1904, Hesse married Maria Bernoulli, a Swiss woman nine years his elder. The couple led an isolated life in Gaienhofen. Sons were born in 1905 and 1909. Hesse was a successful and highly productive writer, but his marriage became progressively less happy. In 1911 he made a journey to the Orient in the company of the painter Hans Sturzenegger. Hesse was particularly interested in India, the country in which both of his parents had lived and which his father and grandfather had studied extensively. The trip, however, did not enable Hesse to find the peace and fulfillment which he so desperately sought. Some of his impressions are recorded in *From India* (1913). His personal conflicts are reflected rather directly in the novel *Rosshalde*, (1914) the story of the painter Johann Veraguth, who lives a lonely and unhappy life at his estate, Rosshalde, with his wife and a younger son, Pierre. An older son, Albert, is away at school and returns only during vacation periods. Life acquires meaning for Veraguth through his work as an artist and his love for Pierre. He tolerates his marriage only for the sake of Pierre. What remains of his happiness is shattered when Pierre dies of meningitis. The end of the novel remains open. Veraguth, turning his back on bourgeois society, leaves Rosshalde and his wife to travel. His future is uncertain.

The outbreak of World War I in 1914 marked another crisis in Hesse's complicated personal life. Although he had been living in Switzerland for many years, he was German and his reading public expected him to support the German cause. (Switzerland remained neutral during the war.) Hesse did not immediately assume an anti-German stand, but he publicly questioned the excessive patriotism in his native country which was brought out by the war and he was in turn sharply criticized from many sides in Germany. He remained in Switzerland throughout the war and was active in the effort to improve the lot of German prisoners of war and internees.

Hesse's literary productivity continued undiminished during the first years of the war and *Knulp*, one of the more popular of his earlier works, appeared in 1915. The three stories contained in the collection will be analyzed in detail in this study guide.

The following year, 1916, was to bring severe misfortune: the death of his father, the serious illness of his son Martin, and the mental breakdown of his wife, who had to be sent to an institution. This was in fact the end of Hesse's first marriage, although he did not obtain a formal divorce until 1923. Hesse was naturally despondent and his search for psychiatric help brought him in contact with Dr. Joseph Lang, a disciple of the eminent psychologist Carl Gustav Jung. From Doctor Lang, Hesse not only received advice which helped him overcome his own personal crisis, but he also learned in detail the theories of Jung. Hesse became a devoted student of Jung and the influence of this psychologist was to become one of the most important factors in his later works.

THE MIDDLE YEARS

Demian was written during a short period of time in 1917 under the immediate influence of Doctor Lang and, through him, of Jung. This new novel marks a radical break in Hesse's literary development and the author did not want his readers in any way to be reminded of his earlier works or to associate the new Hesse - the Hesse of *Demian* - with them. Accordingly he published the novel in 1919 under the pseudonym Emil Sinclair, the name of one of the main characters of the book. The novel was an immediate success. The young postwar generation felt a strong affinity to this strange, powerful work, and it was also well-received by literary critics. The Fontane Prize, a prestigious literary prize awarded for outstanding first novels, was presented to the mysterious Emil Sinclair. The prize was returned by the publisher and in 1920 Hesse revealed that he was actually the author. But he had achieved his goal. To the reading public, Hermann Hesse was now primarily known as the author of *Demian*, not of *Peter Camenzind, Rosshalde*, and other early works which Hesse had come to consider to be immature.

The most important theme of *Demian* is the necessity of first recognizing, and then integrating into one's personality, the two different aspects of life - the "light" and the "dark," the spiritual and the sensual, saintliness and sin. The setting, plot, and style of *Demian* are for the most part dissimilar from those of Hesse's previous works. It is set in Germany during the early years of the present century and describes the outer and inner development of Emil Sinclair from late childhood to maturity. Here, as in *Siddhartha, Narcissus and Goldmund*, and many of Hesse's works - although not in the stories discussed in this study guide - three distinct stages of development can be seen: the early period of innocence, a middle period which is not without searching, loneliness, and even despair, and the final period in which a synthesis is effected. When Emil Sinclair is first introduced to the "dark" world, he sees no way to reconcile the warm, serene atmosphere of his home with the cold frightening world he now sees. But with the help of Max Demian he gradually becomes more and more able to see the possibility of accepting both aspects of his human nature and he eventually finds he is no longer forced to view them as polar opposites.

The year 1919 was indeed an important one. Hesse wrote several important essays during that year, including "Zarathustra's Return" in which his debt to Nietzsche is acknowledged, and three of his better short stories, "A Child's Heart," "Klingsor's Last Summer" and "Klein and Wagner," published together in 1920 under the title *Klingsor's Last Summer*. These three stories will be analyzed in detail in this study guide. Furthermore, Hesse moved from Bern, where he had been living, to the small Swiss town of Montagnola, which was to be his home in his later years. It was also at about this time that Hesse first took up painting; he later became an accomplished painter and it was to remain his favorite hobby throughout his life. And finally, work on the next important book, *Siddhartha*, was begun in this year.

Siddhartha proved to be an especially difficult book to write. As Hesse remarked, the first two periods of the hero's life, those of innocence and searching, were easy for him to portray. But the final triumphant vision of the old Siddhartha was foreign to Hesse's experience and hence he had great difficulty putting it on paper. Only in 1922 was the completed novel published.

In this highly poetic book set in ancient India Hesse describes the life of Siddhartha. First the hero masters his intellect and will, and then he turns to the world of the senses. He finds neither asceticism nor hedonism totally satisfying. Late in life he finds fulfillment in a mystical vision at, and with the help of, a river, the symbol of perfection, unity, and continuity.

In 1923 Hesse became a Swiss citizen. His personal life, however, remained unsettled. He obtained a divorce from his first wife and soon thereafter (in January, 1924) he married Ruth Wenger. Five years were to lapse before the publication of his next major novel, *Steppenwolf* (1927). These years were far from totally barren. Hesse continued to publish poems, short stories, essays, and reviews in various journals and newspapers. But a feeling of alienation, which is reflected in the suffering of Harry Haller in *Steppenwolf*, continued to affect him. His second marriage, like the first, did not prove to be successful; it ended in divorce in 1927. By this time Hesse was one of the most famous writers of his generation and his first full-length biography, by Hugo Ball, appeared in conjunction with his fiftieth birthday in that same year.

Steppenwolf, like *Demian*, "Klein and Wagner," and "Klingsor's Last Summer," has a "realistic" setting in the twentieth century. The hero, Harry Haller, is a middle-aged man who is torn between the world of the bourgeoisie and that of the artist-intellectual. At first he believes that there are but two aspects of his personality, and that he is torn between these irreconcilable poles. He finds a mysterious "treatise" (reflecting insights of his own unconscious) which points out that his conception of a simple duality within himself was incorrect. There are not two Harry Hallers, the Steppenwolf and the bourgeois citizen, but many very different aspects of a complicated individual. Haller gradually comes to realize and accept this fact on a conscious level during the remainder of the novel, and the closing scene, the so-called "Magic Theater," symbolically represents the progress which he has made.

In 1930 one of Hesse's most popular novels appeared, *Narcissus and Goldmund*. Set in the Middle Ages (although not in any specific century), with a plot rich in adventure, the novel examines the duality of spirit and nature, incorporated by the two leading characters, Narcissus and Goldmund, respectively. Most of the story is devoted to Goldmund's wanderings. Originally a seminarian, he is told by his friend and teacher Narcissus that he is not destined for the priesthood. He leaves the seminary and has many adventures. He has brief, but meaningful, affairs with many women; he experiences birth and death, and is himself forced to kill another human being; and great effort he becomes a skilled sculptor and produces a few pieces of extraordinary beauty. Narcissus, on the other hand, becomes a priest and intellectual. Each respects the other, and Narcissus often helps his friend in one way or another. Although Goldmund dies a realistic and un-idealized death, his way of life, which includes both the spirit and the senses, is presented as superior to that of Narcissus, whose philosophy attempts to deny death, and who, as a result, will not be able to face death when it comes, as it inevitably must. In many respects this novel invites comparison with *Knulp*.

Hesse married again in 1931. His third wife, with whom he was to remain until his death some thirty years later, was Ninon Auslander Dolbin. Hesse's happiness during these years is portrayed symbolically in the highly autobiographical, but equally unrealistic, novel *Journey to the East* (1932). The hero is named "H.H.," an obvious allusion to Hermann Hesse, and many other references to the author's life can be detected in the book. Once again the hero goes through three stages in his development. He naively and confidently joins a secret Order or

League and takes part in its "Journey to the East." He later drops out of the League and experiences intense loneliness and despair. With the help of Andreas Leo, a figure who resembles the old Siddhartha in some respects, he finally comes to understand the League, and himself, and then comes to feel a sense of harmony with the world.

For Hesse, unlike most important German-speaking writers, Hitler's rise to power in the early 1930s did not signal any radical changes. Hesse was already a Swiss citizen and although his hatred of war - and of the other things for which Nazism stood-remained undiminished, he was not and never had been a political activist. He had little faith in practical politics and hence did not join the active political opposition to the Nazis. In the early 1930s, under the dark cloud which covered Europe, Hesse began work on his last great novel, *The Glass Bead Game*, or *Magister Ludi*, as it is often called in English. According to Hesse's original plans, this work was to consist of a number of "autobiographies" which would describe successive reincarnations of a single person. Hesse's conception of the novel changed as he was writing it and the emphasis shifted to the final historical period, the world of Castalia, about the year 2400 A.D. The three autobiographies of Joseph Knecht that are appended to the novel are vestiges of the original plan, and a fourth autobiography was also written but not included in the book. As Hesse himself later stated, the writing of *The Glass Bead Game* was his own spiritual defense against the deadly political and moral climate in the world at that time.

Joseph Knecht's biographies and poems, which are appended to the narrator's dry, pedantic biography, most clearly reveal the novel's important issues and themes. Knecht comes to realize that he must seek oneness with nature, but is not able to formulate his ideas, let alone express them adequately and directly in words. He ultimately does realize that he cannot find what he is seeking in the rarified atmosphere of Castalia, and accordingly forsakes it in favor of a life in the "real" world. He dies before coming to a full conscious realization of the significance of his feelings and actions, and critics hence sometimes debate the validity of his life. But he has remained true to himself, and his life must therefore be called successful.

OLD AGE

Hesse's reputation continued to grow after the publication of *The Glass Bead Game*. He was awarded the Nobel Prize for literature - the world's highest literary award-in 1946, and later received several other important prizes and awards in recognition of his literary work. He continued to write poetry and short prose pieces and he faithfully answered the numerous letters addressed to him by admiring readers, although he felt uncomfortable in the role of advisor and father confessor. But *The Glass Bead Game* was to be his last novel. As the years went by, he guarded his privacy more and more carefully and seldom left his secluded home at Montagnola, of which he was so fond. He died of a brain hemorrhage on August 9, 1962, a month after his eighty-fifth birthday.

INTELLECTUAL INFLUENCES

It would be impossible even to list all of the important influences on Hesse. He was exposed to theology, philosophy, literature, and the other arts at an early age and retained his varied interests throughout his long life. Among the literary figures whom he most admired, however, two deserve particular mention: the mystical Romantic poet Novalis (pseudonym of Friedrich von

Hardenberg, 1772-1801), and Johann Wolfgang von Goethe (1749-1832), about whom Hesse once said: "Among all German writers, Goethe is the one to whom I owe the most, the one to whom I am most deeply indebted, who has held my attention, enslaved and encouraged me, forced me to follow his lead or vigorously attack it." Hesse also knew many religious and philosophical writers. As was mentioned above, Christianity was quite important as a formative influence. He also studied various Eastern religions in some depth.

Two of the most important influences on Hesse's thought must be discussed here: the philosopher and poet Friedrich Nietzsche (1844-1900) and the psychologist Carl Gustav Jung (1875-1961). Before going into the extent of these influences, however, it must be emphasized that individuality remained one of Hesse's fundamental values. He read Nietzsche and Jung, as well as Goethe, Novalis, Dostoevski, Freud, and other great writers, but always with a critical eye. Although Hesse did not imitate Nietzsche, Jung, or anyone else, an understanding of certain basic concepts of Nietzsche and Jung can facilitate the approach to some of Hesse's difficult works.

Nietzsche and Jung share some important beliefs which are also to be found in the works of Hesse. Perhaps the most important of these is the insistence upon the necessity of finding one's own path toward self-realization, and of accepting the dark, so-called "sinful" side of human nature in the process. Nietzsche called for a complete revaluation of moral standards entirely eliminating the Judeo-Christian morality which he felt represented a philosophy that valued weakness and conformity rather than strength and individuality, which he preferred. Hesse, too, continually rejects weakness and conformity. The concept which Nietzsche called amor fati ("Love of fate") is likewise shared by Hesse. This concept refers to a joyful acceptance of the world as it is; it is a highly affirmative philosophy, and variations of it can be seen in Klingsor and Klein.

Jung, in more practical terms, refers to the inferior, animalistic side of our nature as the "shadow," and warns against the bad effects of simply attempting to repress it. This part of our human nature must rather be first understood, and then accepted, he maintains. Other of Jung's concepts are also useful in understanding Hesse, especially those of the "unconscious" and the "archetype." Jung believes that a large body of experiences remain in a person's unconscious (he objects to Freud's term "subconscious," which seems to him to carry derogatory implications). Each individual has elements which are part of his "personal unconscious"; that is, memories and emotions from his past which have been removed from his immediate conscious memory, but which may still exert an important and even decisive effect on his behavior unconsciously. There are also elements of the unconscious which are shared by everyone. Jung studied ancient symbols and myths, and analyzed the dreams of his contemporaries. He came to the conclusion that many symbols recur even though modern man may not have known of the ancient representations. Such symbols which have universal significance are said by Jung to be part of the "collective unconscious," and are called "archetypes."

Finally, Jung coined the term "anima" to refer to an unconscious feminine aspect within a man through which he can to some extent intuitively comprehend the nature of women. The references in *Demian* to masculine traits in a woman, or feminine traits in a man, are based on this concept, and many apparent allusions to homosexuality, which some critics are fond of pointing out, can likewise be explained on the basis of Jung's concept. The several aspects of personality, in Jung's formulation, must be integrated if a person, man or woman, is to attain fulfillment. They must accordingly always be considered as parts of a whole, and not as isolated components.

HESSE'S POPULARITY

The history of Hesse's popularity in Germany and America is complex and, on the surface at least, enigmatic. He was a competent popular novelist and essayist during the first two decades of this century and enjoyed a certain following among the German reading public at that time. Upon the publication of *Demian* in 1919, he immediately became one of the heroes of one segment of the younger generation in Germany. His disillusionment with the war and his visionary, even mystical attitude toward the future contributed greatly to his popularity and to his success (although it should be noted that some Germans reproached him for his lack of patriotism during the war). His popularity in German-speaking countries remained high until the early 1930s, when Hitler assumed power in Germany. Because they were largely unpolitical, Hesse's books were not immediately burned and banned in Germany, but his work was not encouraged or even approved by the Nazi hierarchy. Many important intellectuals and writers, both German and non-German, praised Hesse highly. Among these are T.S. Elliot, André Gide, and Thomas Mann. After a brief period of popularity in Europe following the Second World War, Hesse's reputation began to decline, both among academicians and the younger generation of readers. At the present time, Hesse's reputation in Germany is at an all-time low. The young radicals, especially, have no use for his writings since they associate them with the Romantic past - including Nazism! - which they desire to overcome and leave behind.

Hesse has been widely translated into non-European languages, and his reception in India and Japan, especially, has been consistently favorable, and not subject to the ups and downs which mark his popularity in Germany and in America. Hesse was proud of the fact that readers in Eastern countries appreciated his works, which contain many elements of Eastern philosophy.

The history of Hesse's reception in America is quite different from that of his reception in Germany. Although several of his works had appeared in translation throughout the years, he was all but unknown in this country when he received the Nobel Prize for Literature in 1946. The American press for the most part ignored him, even when he received this prestigious award. It was only in the late 1950s that Americans began to become interested in his work. Today, of course, he has become a cult figure. Hesse is without doubt one of the very favorite authors of college-age Americans. Similarly, most of the serious scholarly criticism on Hesse in recent years has been written in English, and most of the important books have been written by North Americans.

It is certainly easy to see why American youth is interested in Hesse. The problems with which he deals in his stories and novels have meaning for young people in this country today. His treatment of adolescence, the problems of growing up, authority, rebellion, the "establishment," sex, human relationships, and, to a lesser extent, drugs, is significant and "relevant." Likewise, many young people share Hesse's interest in Oriental philosophy and in a non-dogmatic theology. It must, however, be pointed out that many important elements of Hesse's thought are overlooked by the majority of his admirers. For example, one often sees a devotion to self-discipline and hard work directed toward the achievement of some specific goal in Hesse's work. Especially

Demian, Siddhartha, and Joseph Knecht attain a remarkable amount of self-discipline while still quite young, and it becomes clear in the respective works that the success and happiness of these characters is possible only because of their earlier rigorous training. If Hesse does not share the Protestant ethic of hard work, he nonetheless sees and portrays in his novels the necessity of building one's life on a firm foundation. Many of his works also show the other side of the coin - the results of not building one's life on a firm foundation (e.g., Klein and Knulp, who is much less happy than the more disciplined wanderer Goldmund). Hesse in no way respects bourgeois narrow-mindedness, complacency, and resistance to change at all cost; but neither does he express approval of destructive rebellion for its own sake. The freedom of Hesse's characters is a reflection of a successful, integrated life; they are slaves neither to tradition nor to their own weaknesses.

It is especially ironic that Hesse has become a folk hero and a model for an entire generation, for Hesse's most important theme throughout his mature works is the necessity of each individual finding his own way in life, rather than following the doctrine or teachings of an authority-figure, however noble or admirable such a figure may be. Often the incidentals of Hesse's novels and stories-rebellion against authority, sexual freedom, etc. - are religiously praised and faithfully followed by his young readers, who thereby completely lose touch with the fundamental aspect of Hesse's thought: the value of an individual's determining, choosing, and continually reexamining his own values. Surely nothing is more foreign to Hesse than the idea that "I have found the way, and there is no other." And this is indeed the narrow-minded philosophy of some of those who have chosen Hesse as their hero and mentor.

It is difficult to predict what direction Hesse's future popularity will take. More and more of his works are being translated into English - short stories, essays on various subjects, poems, autobiographical sketches, indeed almost anything will be eagerly purchased by his faithful reading public. Sooner or later a reaction must take place. Much of Hesse's short prose fiction is not especially rich or rewarding; his essays are to a great extent dated and have only historical interest; his range as a poet is narrow and poetry is in any event difficult to translate, or to appreciate in translation; and his autobiographical works are unquestionably among his least successful. It is to be hoped that these minor works will enable the American reader to more fully appreciate the complexity of Hesse, without detracting from his truly great novels and short stories.

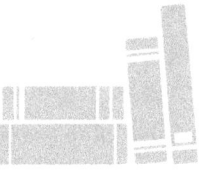

DEMIAN

GENRE, STYLE AND CENTRAL THEME

Genre. *Demian* is immediately recognizable as belonging to a very specific species of novel, the Bildungsroman (Novel of Personal Development). A characteristically German form of the novel, and Germany's chief contribution to the evolution of the European novel, the Bildungsroman traditionally traces the development of a youth from a tabula rasa-like state of naive ignorance to the attainment of wisdom, the integration of his personality, and the full realization of all his latent capabilities. This process usually takes place with the aid of an older spiritual guide or mentor who has already reached the goal toward which the hero strives. The wisdom attained, furthermore, represents the highest ideals of the period in which the particular Bildungsroman was written. Unlike the English, French, and Russian novel of manners, the Bildungsroman does not emphasize social milieu and the smoothly flowing narrative of a tightly woven plot. In emphasizing, instead, the subjective development of the hero, the Bildungsroman concentrates episodically on (and derives its coherence from) only those experiences of the hero which are important milestones in his development. It was in the modernization of these traditional Bildungsroman elements that Hesse was able to give *Demian* its contemporary appeal. In the first place, the ideal wisdom which the hero Emil Sinclair strives to attain with the aid of his mentor Max Demian has a characteristically twentieth-century flavor in that it has been completely internalized and made individual, subjective, and above all existential. Secondly, this ideal wisdom and the process of its attainment are presented through the medium of myths and symbols seen in the light of modern depth psychology.

Style. It is virtually impossible to discuss the style of a piece of literature when one is dealing with a translation rather than the original (it being assumed here that this study is primarily for those who will be reading *Demian* in English), for as Mark Boulby rightly remarks in his book on Hesse (see **bibliography**), "The deceptive simplicity of much of Hesse's prose disguises the fact that at its best it is untranslatable because of its strong lyrical tonal qualities." Boulby's view is supported by Ralph Freedman's book, *The Lyrical Novel*, which devotes a chapter to Hesse. Nevertheless, a few general remarks about the style of *Demian* can be attempted.

The first and most obvious stylistic fact about *Demian* is that it is written in the first person. Hesse has dispensed with the traditional external omniscient narrator who would tell us objectively about Emil Sinclair. Instead, everything is seen from the inside, we are made parties to Sinclair's subjectivity, and we see the world only as he sees it. Sinclair mentions only those things that have importance to him in his personal growth. Max Demian and Demian's mother, Frau Eva, loom large in the novel, for instance, but Sinclair's own mother (and his father and sisters as well) hardly exist at all. Objectively, one would expect Sinclair's family to take precedence over outsiders, but subjectively, from the point of view of Sinclair's development, Demian and Frau Eva are simply more important, so Sinclair dwells on them at the expense of his closest relatives. In the same way, the external environment is shadowy and vague. We learn very little about the town where Sinclair grows up and of the other places where he stays; and, more importantly, we learn nothing about Sinclair's appearance. The latter is stylistically appropriate, as we are not looking at Sinclair from the outside and thus "seeing" him. We are, rather, inside of Sinclair and we do not see him anymore than he can see himself. The lack of objective information as to Sinclair's appearance has the added advantage that the reader can more easily identify with and internally assimilate the hero, for everyone is left to imagine for himself what Sinclair looks like.

Interiorization is a progressive process in *Demian*. The more Sinclair develops as the novel unfolds, the more internal reality takes precedence over external reality. In the first part of the novel Sinclair experiences external reality first, and only then is its inner meaning revealed symbolically to him (usually in a dream). At the end of the novel, however, in Sinclair's climactic vision, the inner, symbolic reality is given first, and only later do we realize that there was an objective, external basis for his mystical experience: an exploding bombshell. The juxtaposition of external, objective and internal, subjective (or of the mundane and the mystical, symbolic realms) constitutes one of the chief stylistic features of *Demian*. In depicting a world in which two levels of reality exist side by side, Hesse has succeeded in imparting to the pages of his novel an indescribable but unmistakable sense of an all-pervading mysterious surrealism.

Underlying the subjectivity of the novel is Sinclair's (Hesse's) passionate will to self-expression, to a self-expression concerned only with the essence of things, the absolute, the soul. *Demian* is utterly serious, it takes itself seriously, and it is completely lacking in that wonderful irony and self-effacing humor that is a characteristic feature of Hesse's later work (after *Siddhartha*). In these attributes of *Demian* there is a stylistic affinity with the spirit of Expressionism which was the literary vogue in Germany at the time of the novel's conception.

Because of its subjectivity, its fervent self-expression, its high seriousness and pathos, *Demian* has all the earmarks of a confession (in the technical, literary sense of a spiritual autobiography) in the tradition of Augustine, Rousseau, and the Romantics. Since all of Hesse's works are highly autobiographical, the present novel not excluded, *Demian* can be called, in a sense, Hesse's confession.

To what degree, if at all, Hesse may have had Augustine or Rousseau in mind when writing *Demian* is not known. It is known, however, that there are two specific stylistic models for the novel which greatly influenced the tone of its language. These are Nietzsche's *Thus Spake Zarathustra* (1883-1892) and the Bible. These models add to the seriousness, if not heaviness, of the style and give it a supra-personal (remember: Sinclair is not only an individual, but the symbolic representation of his whole generation) prophetic and proclamatory ring. The language of *Demian* is full of mystical, theological and mythological symbols on the one hand and Nietzschean vigor on the other. The Bible and Nietzsche (that great hater of Christianity) make strange bedfellows (even though Zarathustra itself is highly Biblical in style), and this contributes to what Ziolkowski calls the stylistic tension of the novel: "Hesse creates a conscious stylistic tension by pitting Christian phraseology against Nietzschean thought, whereby the tone of the book becomes decidedly religious" (*The Novels of Hermann Hesse*).

In summary, the chief stylistic characteristics of *Demian* may be briefly listed as follows:

1. **tonally rich and lyrical**

2. **subjective, progressively interiorized**

3. **surrealistic**

4. **fervently self-expressive, confessional**

5. **utterly serious, lacking in humor and irony**

6. **rich in pathos**

7. **rich in Biblical tonalities, full of mystic, theological, and mythological symbolism**

8. **Nietzschean**

9. **supra-personal in a prophetic, proclamatory sense**

10. **productive of tension between the Biblical, Christian and the Nietzschean, anti-Christian.**

THE CENTRAL THEME

The mere determining of the genre of *Demian* as a Bildungsroman already tells us that the central theme of the novel must be the inner development of its hero, Emil Sinclair. But since it is a modernized Bildungsroman, that development will take place within the context of the contemporary existential issues of Angst, the relation of the individual to society, the fragmentation of modern man, the question of morality, and the quest for identity. *Demian* is thus the story of Emil Sinclair's search for himself as he goes through the stages of original innocence, guilt, alienation, despair to the eventual attainment of totality and unity - stages which correspond exactly to the three steps in the quest for identity as outlined by Hesse in "A Little Bit of Theology". Underlying Sinclair's whole existence is the problem of duality and the search for synthesis. Sinclair must and does come to see that "darkness," evil, and the abyss, are not "out there" in the world, but within him as a part of his own soul. His task is thus to reject all systems which deny, suppress, or ignore the "lower half" of human nature (i.e. conventional morality) and to struggle to find his own philosophy which will embrace all of life, the total man, both his "light" and his "dark" sides. The acceptance of his total personality instead of merely one officially sanctioned half of his nature, and the creation of his own system of values does not mean that Sinclair becomes a champion of moral chaos. Rather, the acknowledgment of forbidden desires is the necessary precondition for their reshaping into meaningful, productive drives. To put it in terms of depth psychology, it is not the suppression of "the devil within us" (Jung calls it the "Shadow") that is the hallmark of true morality, but the integration, the sublimation, of the "Shadow."

THE MAJOR CHARACTERS (ARRANGED IN ORDER OF APPEARANCE)

Emil Sinclair

The name Sinclair is probably taken from Isaak von Sinclair (1775-1815), the German author, philosopher, and courtier who was the great friend and benefactor of Friedrich Holderlin (1770-1843), one of the poets most admired by Hesse. It has also been suggested that Sinclair can be seen as a compound of the English word "sin" and the French word "clair" (light). As such the name alludes to the two worlds of the novel, the two sides of Sinclair's nature, which he seeks to reconcile, the "dark" world of sin, forbidden desires, etc., and the "light" world of spirituality and goodness. As far as the first name, Emil, is concerned, perhaps Hesse had Rousseau's novel of education, Emile, in mind, the basic idea of which would fit Demian's slant, namely that education should be self-development, free self-expression, rather than conformity to an a priori external model induced through constraint. (See Joseph Mileck, "Names and the Creative Process," in the bibliography.)

Although there are no dates mentioned in the novel, it is obvious that it ends at the outbreak of World War I. Using 1914 as a guidepost, one can deduce quite easily that *Demian* is the first-person narrative of the life of Emil Sinclair during the crucial years of growing up, from the ages of around ten to twenty. The novel is set, then, roughly in the last decade of peace before the First World War (c. 1904-1914).

Emil Sinclair, the sensitive son of an upper-middle-class family living in an unspecified German town, gradually becomes conscious of the spiritual and moral disparities and contradictions in his environment. Through his own bitter experiences at the hands of the bully Franz Kromer, and as a result of the unheard-of teachings on life, morality, and theology imparted to him by his friend and example Max Demian, Sinclair's unquestioned faith in the moral authority of his parents, teachers, religion, and the "establishment" in general, is thoroughly shaken. On his way through grade school and high school, Sinclair engages in a fervent and often erring search for the meaning of life, for something to take the place of his now-rejected conventional values. During this period a new friend, Pistorius, supplements Demian's teaching by showing Sinclair that he must recognize only inner reality and that he must walk alone, regardless of where this might lead.

At university Sinclair meets Frau Eva, Demian's mother. He sees in her the embodiment of his great dream of a "mother of all being," the living symbol of integration and resolution of all contradictions and opposites. She becomes for Sinclair simultaneously the object of his erotic desire as well as the object of his filial and even religious devotion. Under the influence of Frau Eva and Demian, Sinclair's development reaches a mature stage where he is "beyond good and evil," where he has begun to accept and integrate the warring forces of "light" and "darkness" within him. Before Sinclair can consummate his love for Frau Eva, the Great War breaks out. At the front Sinclair experiences the horrors of war, but believes the fighting to be the birth pangs of a new humanity, the dawning of a new age of the spirit to supplant the bankrupt morality of the pre-war era. Wounded, Sinclair ends up lying next to Demian in a field hospital. Demian dies there, but not before transmitting to Sinclair Frau Eva's final blessing. Demian is gone and Frau Eva is distant, but Sinclair now realizes that he no longer needs them (or any other outside mentors) because he has internalized their essence. Fully autonomous and at one with himself, Sinclair decides to write the story of his way to wholeness.

Franz Kromer

It is interesting to note that Hesse has given Franz Kromer the first name of his once-favorite saint, St. Francis of Assisi, about whom he wrote an admiring essay in 1904 (Francis of Assisi).

Perhaps Hesse was trying to indicate here, in *Demian*, his rejection of his pre-war literary phase (in which St. Francis was venerated) by giving the saint's name to the mean bully. At any rate, Franz Kromer (although only a boy) is a devil figure, the personification of evil, the embodiment of the Jungian "Shadow" (the "dark" side of the psyche, the enemy of the best in us), and a representative of that forbidden lower-class world of scandal, violence, and lawlessness which the proper and respectable Sinclair fears, yet to which he feels attracted.

Franz Kromer is responsible for the first crisis in Sinclair's life, his "fall from paradise," i.e. his loss of blissful childhood innocence. One day, the two boys happened to meet under a bridge, and Franz began bragging about his bold exploits. Afraid he would evoke Kromer's contempt if he did not have an anecdote of his own to narrate, Sinclair told of having stolen apples from a neighbor's garden. Although Sinclair's story is a fabrication, invented out of fear of Kromer, Franz is able to use the tale to blackmail Sinclair into giving him money stolen from his parents in order to keep Kromer from turning him in. The lie, the theft from his parents, his now having a secret to hide from them, all create such strong guilt feelings in Sinclair that he feels separated from his family, an outcast in his own home. His life under Kromer's thumb is utter misery until he is finally released by the intervention of a new friend, Max Demian.

With Demian's help, Sinclair later learns an important lesson from this episode. He learns that evil is not a purely external phenomenon existing solely in Kromer, or in the world he represents. He learns that evil exists within himself as well. It was he who lied, he who was too weak, or too proud, to undercut Kromer's blackmail by immediately confiding in his parents, he who stole, he who in this way cooperated with Kromer, or, as he says, "gave the devil his hand." This insight represents one of the first steps in Sinclair's process of progressive introspection and self-illumination.

Max Demian

If Franz Kromer is the embodiment of the Jungian "Shadow," Demian is the symbol of Jung's "Self." According to Jung, the Self is both the center and the circumference of the psyche. Embracing the totality of the person, both in its conscious and unconscious aspects, the Self represents the origin and goal of "individuation" (self-realization, or psychic integration) based on the union or synthesis of all of life's polarities, good and evil, outward and inward reality, spirit and body, etc. It is Demian's status as realized Self-hood that Hesse attempts to depict (and Demian is the most fully described character in the novel) by giving him attributes symbolic of totality. Demian seems ageless; youth, maturity and old age are blended in his features in a timeless synthesis. The inorganic and organic realms seem united in him when his face takes on the appearance of a stone statue, or better, idol. (One is reminded of statues of Buddha, another symbol of the Self.) Also, the animal and human kingdoms seem united at times in Demian's features. The union of opposites is also expressed with sexual symbolism when Demian is described as having hermaphroditic features. Demian's mind seems fully in control of his body. He can go into deep trance at will, and he can even influence the actions of others by merely exercising his uncanny will power. Of course, he is totally self-sufficient; also, he is possessed of inexplicable knowledge of arcane philosophies and theologies. None of this is ever explained. He remains an enigma, a mystery as much as the human psyche itself ultimately is. Demian is totally unique, yet he immediately recognizes a kindred soul in Emil Sinclair who has all the potential, given some gentle guidance, to someday also attain Self-hood. In his role as teacher he never obtrudes himself upon Sinclair. He is kind and gentle, ever respectful of Sinclair's individuality and personal integrity. He is the perfect tutor who guides by example and never pushes.

Demian does seem Buddha-like in his stone-faced trances, but he also has a strong resemblance to another great religious teacher, Christ:

1. **Demian is a moral and spiritual teacher.**

2. **He teaches in parables.**

3. **He has a halo-like glow about him.**

4. **The status of his father is unclear.**

5. **He saves Sinclair from the "devil" Franz Kromer.**

6. **He talks of a new religio-spiritual kingdom of the soul for which mankind must prepare.**

7. **He has a circle of disciples.**

8. **He says in dying that he will always be with Sinclair spiritually, even though physically absent.**

9. **In the last sentence of the novel the pronoun referring to Demian is capitalized twice.**

In spite of these Christ-like attributes, however, there is no getting around the fact that the content of Demian's teaching is anything but Christian. "[Demian] is...the mouthpiece of the Nietzschean goal [i.e. transvaluation of all values, superman life beyond good and evil, amor fati] toward which Sinclair is striving, and that is his most significant contextual function in the novel" (Ziolkowski, *The Novels of Hermann Hesse*).

It is usually assumed that the name Demian alludes to the Greek daimon, the inner voice which, according to Socrates, guides and awakens the soul of the truth seeker, a function which would certainly fit Demian's role in the novel.

In a letter of December 1955, Hesse had something interesting to reveal about the name which fits into the character of the novel like a hand in a glove: "The name 'Demian' is not something I chose or invented. It came to me in a dream and appealed to me so strongly that I put it on the title of my book." Hesse was living in Montagnola in Italian Switzerland at the time the novel was written and there does exist an Italian family-name Demiani, so perhaps Hesse had heard the name, forgotten it, and "remembered" it in his dreams.

Pistorius

Pistorius has a very specific and essential function to perform at a crucial phase in Sinclair's development, after which he is dispensed with, both in the sense that Hesse gives him no further place in the novel, and in the sense that Sinclair terminates their friendship. It is Pistorius' role to introduce Sinclair to the world of myths, symbols and archetypes by means of which he helps him to understand the frequent dreams which have been troubling him at this stage in his life. He teaches Sinclair that these dreams are the voice of his collective unconscious, that is, that they are not personal in origin but that they are symbolic manifestations of universal human problems of spiritual growth. Of course this does not mean that the dreams do not have profound significance for Sinclair's development as an individual. It is because they are archetypal not in spite of the fact, that the dreams are important for Sinclair, Pistorius avers. In short, Pistorius helps Sinclair to raise the contents of his unconscious to the level of consciousness and rational meaning, the only level on which what he has now learned are the vast depths of his soul can be acknowledged, appreciated, and assimilated - a process essential for the attainment of self-realization.

Pistorius plays much the same role in Sinclair's life as did Dr. J. B. Lang, the Jungian psychiatrist, in Hesse's life. As a matter of fact, Pistorius is modeled after Dr. Lang, with whom Hesse spent many sessions in 1916-1917. Dr. Lang is also actually referred to as "Pistorius" in Hesse's Journey to Nurnberg (1927).

The name Pistorius is simply the Latin form of the common German surname Backer (Baker). It was not uncommon in the Renaissance period in Germany for the humanists to translate their names into Latin or Greek. Pistorius' Latinized name, with its Renaissance and classical allusions, gives him some of the aura of antiquity and learning which befits his character. There actually was, furthermore, a well-known sixteenth-century theologian from Baden, near Hesse's home area, called Johann Pistorius. Hesse's Pistorius, of course, studied theology.

Pistorius is somewhat of an eccentric. The son of a pastor, and a divinity student who dropped out of university before formally concluding his studies, he lives the life of a recluse in the converted garret of his father's house. He makes a modest living as an organist at a small church and likes to go there alone at night to meditate while playing Bach and Buxtehude. Next to music (and wine - Pistorius has alcoholic tendencies) his great love is mythology and the history of religions. He is steeped in the esoteric lore of forgotten cults. Pistorius' main fault, and the reason for Sinclair's leaving him, is that he ignores the present and lives in the past. He is a romantic antiquarian. There is something dusty and museal about him, he lacks vigor and vitality. He cannot apply to his own life the helpful psychological insights that he passes on to Sinclair, and so Pistorius does not grow or develop. He is static rather than dynamic.

Frau Eva

Frau Eva, Demian's mother, is not as important as a person in her own right, or objective character in the novel, as she is as what she represents to Sinclair. Thus she will be discussed under the heading "The Major Symbols," below.

THE MAJOR SYMBOLS

Abraxas

During Sinclair's troubled years at boarding school, the period when he meets Pistorius and is bothered by strange dreams, he paints from memory a picture of the ancient crest carved over the entrance of his father's house, a crest he had once seen Demian sketching years before. It is the picture of a bird of prey sitting upon some object which can no longer be determined. Sinclair likes the painting so much he mails it to Demian. Later he receives a cryptic note from his friend containing the following comments on the painting: "The bird is struggling out of the egg. The egg is the world. Whoever wishes to be born must destroy a world. The bird is flying to God. The God is Abraxas." Sinclair had never heard of a god named Abraxas before, but Doctor Follen, his classics teacher, explains the meaning of the name to him: "We can think of the name more or less as that of a deity who has the symbolic task of uniting the divine and the satanic." Doctor Follen's words are reminiscent of a remark Demian had once made to Sinclair when they were in confirmation class together: "I have nothing against honoring this God Jehova.... But I think we should honor everything and hold it sacred, the whole world, not just this artificially separated, official half. Therefore we ought to have worship of the devil as well as worship of God." There is something in Sinclair, Demian is suggesting here, that will hinder his development. It is the influence of the Christian God in whom the world of "light" and goodness has its highest symbol: This God recognizes only one half of the world, as it were, so that one finds it necessary to hide the other half from Him. But this other "forbidden" half of the world (Demian is alluding to such things as man's sexuality, his will to power and untrammelled self-expression, etc.) belongs to man's nature just as much as the sanctioned portion of reality does. Thus a life led in the exclusive service of the God of "light" is a lie, Demian argues, because it suppresses or denies one half of man's nature and at that, the half which it is essential to develop if one is going to attain self-realization. Thus the one-sided God arrests man's development. The soul which wants to realize its potential, attain totality, and achieve a union of spirit and nature, is in need of a god who is himself a symbol not just of "light" but of totality, of "light" and "darkness." Such a god is Abraxas. In short, then, in spite of all the theological wording, Abraxas, as an encompassor of opposites, is nothing but another of Hesse's recurrent symbols of totality and unity.

There actually was a god called Abraxas worshipped by certain Gnostic sects as a symbol of totality. In numerology each letter of the alphabet was assigned a certain number. The numeric value of the letters in the name Abraxas totaled 365, the number of days in the year. Furthermore, the seven letters of the name signified the seven heavens of the Gnostics. There is even a precedent in German literature for using the name. In his poetic cycle Western-Eastern Divan, Goethe refers to Abraxas twice. But these matters were really not of primary interest to Hesse. Abraxas' chief function in *Demian* is simply that of a totality symbol. But if this is true, it still could be asked, why use Abraxas at all, why not some other, less obscure symbol? The following answers could be given to this question:

1. The use of the name of a god to signify totality fits in with Hesse's conviction that the search for self-realization is ultimately a religious quest.

2. The use of a pagan god allows Hesse to indicate that in his opinion Christianity hinders rather than helps self-realization. It might be added in this context that Hesse's view of Christianity was unwittingly prejudiced. The Christianity he knew best, nineteenth-century Protestantism, was a distorted Christianity having little in common with the original church. What Hesse and so many German intellectuals of Protestant upbringing were reacting against was not the orthodox faith (which they strangely ignored) but a "Christianity" that was really nothing more than Neo-Platonism, with its over-emphasis on the "spiritual" at the expense of the physical and its resultant neglect of liturgy, sacraments, and the dogmas of Incarnation and Resurrection of the Body, all aspects of orthodoxy based, ironically, on that very synthesis of spirit and matter which Hesse thought he could find only by denying the church.

3. The use of a specifically Gnostic god (gnosis means knowledge in Greek) instead of some other pagan deity alludes to the fact that Sinclair's "salvation" is acquired

by knowledge, rather than by some other means (Hesse later called this knowledge "magical thinking," by which he meant the ability to discern unity or totality underlying the apparent contradictions and polarities in the world).

Beatrice

By the middle of the novel, Sinclair still has not been able to decide which direction his life should take. Due to the influences of the Kromer episode, Demian's teachings, and the onslaught of sexual awakening, Sinclair left the "light" world of his childhood innocence and parental home only to find himself in a spiritual vacuum with nothing to prevent him from swinging, now, to the opposite pole, to the "dark" world of alienation and debauchery. But, as Holderlin once wrote, "Where there is danger, /The powers of deliverance grow too." Thus it is precisely at this critical nadir that Sinclair encounters the catalyst which will set loose the psychic powers of his spiritual regeneration. That catalyst is Beatrice, and from the time he discovers her, Sinclair's life is no longer a pendulation between extremes but an intensification of his search for himself.

Who is Beatrice, and how can she have such a profound effect upon Sinclair? He never meets her, never talks to her, never learns anything about her. He only sees her when out walking. These objective things are not important, however. Her significance lies solely in what she means to Sinclair subjectively, and that meaning is contained in the name he gives her, Beatrice, the name of the "heavenly, beloved one" in the Divine Comedy, and since Dante's time a symbol of spiritual purity. In typical fashion, Hesse has taken, here, a traditional symbol and used it in a modern way by making its function in Sinclair's life psychological and existential. At a time when Sinclair has reached bottom there begin to stir within his psyche the rallying forces of recovery: "...no need, no urge, was so deep and vehement within me," Sinclair says, "as the wish for reverence and devotion!" What these psychic forces need is a form of expression, and objectification, a symbol, something empirical and external for Sinclair to experience and assimilate consciously. And this is Beatrice. "Suddenly I had an image before me again," Sinclair says of her, "a lofty and revered image... I had, now, something to love and to venerate."

Jung's term for this process is "projection." Unconscious contents of the psyche are "projected" onto an appropriate something or someone in the environment which (or who) is then "discovered" there by the conscious subject and reassimilated to his benefit. In Jungian terms, Beatrice is the projection of the archetype of purity. Sinclair, who now has "something to love and to venerate" in Beatrice, senses this intuitively when he says that the new "world of light" in which he now lives (since seeing Beatrice he has completely reformed) has its origin within him: "...the new 'world of light' was more or less my own creation,... it was a new devotion which I invented and demanded, replete with responsibility and self-discipline" (italics supplied).

Beatrice is a means rather than an end. Her function as a catalyst is to set in motion the healing forces deep within Sinclair, after which she fades from his mind. Once projected and reassimilated, her function is at an end, the initiated momentum of Sinclair's inner development takes its course. This is shown when Sinclair attempts to paint Beatrice and unwittingly ends up painting Demian and Frau Eva instead. New projections are now incubating in Sinclair's psyche. It is interesting to note in this context that Beatrice anticipates to a degree the ultimate projection, Frau Eva. There is an indication that Beatrice, like

Frau Eva, has hermaphroditic qualities, symbolic of totality, for the boyishness of her appearance is emphasized.

The Bird And The Egg

"The symbol of the bird and the egg,..." says Theodore Ziolkowski (*The Novels of Hermann Hesse*), "is the central symbol of [*Demian*]. Introduced almost on the first page, it is maintained to the very end. But whereas in the first half of the novel it is a personal symbol, it assumes universal proportions in the second part."

We first meet the symbol in **chapter two** when Max Demian calls Sinclair's attention to the ancient crest carved over the portal of Sinclair's house. It is a weather-beaten and now indistinct coat of arms, but Demian discerns in it the picture of a bird. "I believe that it is a sparrow hawk," he tells Sinclair.

The image figures next in **chapter four**. Sinclair is trying to remember when it was that he first met Demian and he recalls that it was the time when they were standing before Sinclair's house and Demian had pointed out the heraldic bird. That night Sinclair dreams of the crest and he spends the next few days painting it from memory as best he can. He describes the final version of his picture in this way: "Now it was a bird-of-prey with a sharp, bold sparrow hawk's head. With half its body it was sticking out of a dark earth-sphere, out of which it was struggling to free itself as if out of a gigantic egg, on a background of blue sky." Pleased with his work, Sinclair mails the painting to Demian.

In **chapter five**, called "The Bird Struggles out of the Egg," Sinclair gets a strange answer from Demian in thanks for being sent the picture. It is a cryptic note commenting on the painting's meaning: "The bird is struggling out of the egg. The egg is the world. Whoever wants to be born must destroy a world. The bird is flying to God. The God is Abraxas."

In chapter seven, next to the last chapter, Sinclair is now at university and has found Demian there. It is their first reunion in many years. Upon his first visit to Demian's home, he is ushered into the hall by a maid and left alone there for a moment. He looks up at a door and sees hanging there, carefully framed, his painting of the bird. A moment later Frau Eva, Demian's mother, appears in the door to greet him. This is the first time Sinclair has ever seen Frau Eva, and there she is, standing under his picture.

The symbol is mentioned again at the end of chapter seven. It is now the summer of 1914, immediately prior to the outbreak of the war. Sinclair is walking in the countryside when storm clouds begin to form. In their turbulent contours Sinclair sees the shape of a giant bird tearing itself loose from the blue-grey chaos and disappearing into the sky. Then a violent thunder-and-hail storm breaks out. Sinclair later relates this experience to Demian and tells him that for a moment he clearly saw an image in the clouds, the image of a bird. When Demian asks if it was a sparrow hawk, Sinclair answers: "Yes, it was my sparrow hawk. It was yellow [in the painting the bird is yellow] and gigantic, and it flew into the blue-black sky."

The bird symbol occurs, finally, in the last chapter of the book. Sinclair, now a soldier at the front, is reflecting upon his interpretation of the war as the hour of birth of a new humanity and he closes his thoughts with this idea: "Our primordial feelings, even the wildest ones, were not directed at the enemy. The bloody work of these feelings was only an expression of something inside of us, of our soul, torn asunder and at odds with itself. This soul wanted to rage and kill, destroy and die, in order to be born new. A giant bird is struggling out of the egg, and the egg was the world, and the world had to be destroyed."

Essential to the interpretation of this important symbol are the following points:

1. Birds are a very ancient symbol of the soul. In the Bible for instance, to mention but one example, we read in the 124th psalm, verse 6: "Our soul is escaped even as a bird out of the snare of the fowler. The snare is broken, and we are delivered."

2. Sinclair himself says in the description of his picture that the egg out of which the bird is struggling is the world. The idea of the egg as a symbol of the world comes from the Swiss anthropologist J. J. Bachofen (1815-1887; see discussion of Bachofen below). In a chapter entitled "The Egg as Symbol," in his Essay on Grave Symbolism of the Ancients (1859), Bachofen wrote about symbolic eggs depicted on the ancient tombs at the Villa Pamfilia in Rome. Each egg was light on top and dark on the bottom. Bachofen interpreted this as symbolizing "the perpetual transition from darkness to light, from death to life," and as standing for "tellurian creation as the result of an eternal coming into being and an eternal perishing, as a never-ending motion between opposite poles."

3. If we add to these ideas of Bachofen's the fact that according to Demian the bird is breaking out of its world-egg in order to fly to that symbol of totality, Abraxas (the combination of bird-world-egg symbolism with Abraxas is, incidentally, Hesse's own idea), then

the meaning of this complicated symbol becomes clear: The bird breaking out of the world-egg to fly to Abraxas represents Sinclair's soul in its struggle to free itself from the traditional world with its dichotomies of "good" and "evil," "light" and "darkness," etc., in order to rise to a new level of totality, of synthesis of opposites, "beyond good and evil." That would be the personal meaning of the symbol, as far as Sinclair is concerned. But when he sees the bird in the clouds on the eve of World War I (it is clear, of course, that the thunderstorm is symbolic of the outbreak of war), and in view of his evocation of the bird symbol again at the front, the image also represents Western man struggling to break out of the traditional bonds of a moribund civilization of false polarities.

4. It is significant that Sinclair's bird is not just any bird, not, for instance, a dove, but a noble bird, a sparrow hawk. The species of bird chosen to represent Sinclair's soul symbolizes his aristocratic status as a member of a spiritual elite of seekers of self-realization bearing the distinction of the mark of Cain (see below). As such Sinclair is above the common mass, the "sparrows," of humanity.

5. Sinclair's painting of the bird and the egg provides an interesting illustration of the workings of Jung's concept of the collective unconscious. After dreaming of the bird (dreams are, according to Jung, one of the prime manifestations of the unconscious), Sinclair paints it. He does not know what the object was upon which the original bird was resting in the crest over his father's portal. Yet Sinclair paints it emerging out of a world-egg, and thus he unconsciously but meaningfully links his

painting to ancient cult symbolism as rediscovered by Bachofen.

6. It is worth noting that the picture of the bird is associated with doors. It is situated over the entrance to Sinclair's house, and it also hangs over a door in Demian's home. Now doors are symbols of passage, of transition from one state to another. The positioning of the bird over doors adds to its symbolic meaning as the icon of Sinclair's pilgrimage from a state of fragmentation to the wholeness of Self-hood.

Frau Eva

Frau Eva is Sinclair's living symbol of integration, of the resolution of all contradictions and opposites, the embodiment of his destiny, the fulfillment of all his ideals, and the culmination of an ascending series of symbolic images (Beatrice, Demian, Abraxas) marking Sinclair's road to self-realization. She is also, as her name Eve indicates, the magna mater, the archetypal Great Mother of man, out of whose body is born a new humanity in Sinclair's mystical vision at the end of the book.

Two aspects of great importance to the discussion of this key symbol are the incest motif, and the development of Frau Eva as a projected image of Sinclair's psyche.

1. Incest Motif. By dint of her symbolic name, Frau Eva is by definition mother. "What a wonderful mother you have," Sinclair tells Demian, "Frau Eva! The name fits her completely, she is the mother of all being." Thus the erotic love Sinclair has for her is incestuous in a way. This is stated quite explicitly by Sinclair on the day he learns Frau Eva's name. "From this day on," Sinclair

says, "I went in and out of [Frau Eva's and Demian's] house like a son and brother, but also like a lover."

Sinclair first encounters Frau Eva, significantly enough, in a dream, and that dream is clearly incestuous. Sinclair dreams he is embracing his mother, but as he does so she changes into someone else, "a figure I had never seen before, large and powerful, resembling Max Demian and my painting, but yet different, and in spite of her power completely feminine." (Sinclair does not yet know who this woman is, but later it becomes clear that it was Frau Eva.) The maternal embrace soon turns into an intense erotic caress. Sinclair feels guilty about this dream because, as he says, too much of his mother was still spooking in the figure for the embrace not to seem terribly sinful, i.e. incestuous. The importance of this dream should not be underestimated. It is, after all, Sinclair's first encounter with the Great Mother archetype. Sinclair says of it: "This dream [was] the most important one of my life and the one with the most lasting effect." At a later time, Sinclair dreams, symbolically, of sexual union with Frau Eva: "She was an ocean into which I flowed like a river," he says.

Although Sinclair does have real feelings of erotic as well as filial love for Frau Eva, the significance of the incest motif in *Demian* is symbolic rather than literal. Depth psychology has shown the incest motif (as it occurs in myths for example) to be a common symbolic expression of the death-rebirth archetype. The renewal of the individual, his "rebirth," is brought about by returning to the origin and source of life, symbolized archetypally by the magna mater, the Great Mother, Eve if one will. One's return to the womb of life is symbolized by the act of incest in which one, in sexual union with the mother, sires oneself in order to be born anew. The incest motif in *Demian*, thus, symbolizes Sinclair's renewal, the "death" of his old fragmented self, and the "rebirth" of the new Sinclair of attained self-realization.

2. Development of Frau Eva as Image. Three important facets of the development of Frau Eva as a projected image of Sinclair's psyche are: (a) The identification of Frau Eva with Abraxas, (b) Sinclair's internalization of the projected symbol, and (c) the universalization of the symbol to stand for the rebirth not only of Sinclair, but of all Western civilization as well.

(a) Frau Eva's importance lies in the fact that she symbolizes the union of opposites. To name but two examples of this, she is capable of being, simultaneously, the object of opposite kinds of love, the filial, Platonic, and the erotic, and her features are often described as an androgynous combination of masculine and feminine qualities. In other words, Frau Eva, in symbolizing the synthesis of dualisms, has exactly the same characteristics as does Abraxas, the god who unites good and evil, the "light" and the "dark" worlds. The essential identity of Frau Eva and Abraxas only dawns on Sinclair slowly. After that initial incestuous dream (discussed above) Sinclair relates: "Only gradually and unconsciously did a connection occur to me between this completely inner image [i.e. the woman in the dream] and... [Abraxas]. This connection became closer and more intimate, however, and I began to feel that specifically in this premonitive dream I was calling upon Abraxas. Rapture and horror, man and woman mixed together, the sacred and the atrocious interwoven, trembling with deep guilt and most tender innocence - thus was the image in my dream, and thus also was Abraxas."

Sinclair is so obsessed with the woman in his dream that he decides to paint her. The painting becomes a kind of strange icon for him: "I questioned the picture, I accused it, I caressed it, I prayed to it; I called it mother, I called it beloved, called it whore and slut, called it Abraxas."

(We soon learn that the image of Sinclair's dream, the image he paints, is indeed Frau Eva. While he is on a visit home from school for the holidays, the landlady of the house where Demian used to live shows Sinclair a photograph of Frau Eva. "As I now looked at that little likeness," Sinclair relates, "my heart stood still. That was the image of my dream!")

The culmination of the series of equations between Frau Eva and Abraxas comes when Sinclair meets Frau Eva for the first time. The context of this meeting is very significant, for when Sinclair first lays eyes on Frau Eva she is standing in the doorway directly beneath Sinclair's picture of the bird breaking out of the egg to fly to Abraxas. In this scene the whole complex of symbols comes to lucid fruition. The doorway in which Frau Eva stands symbolizes passage, transition from one state to another. She is the way; her standing in the door says this symbolically. The bird of the picture is, of course, Sinclair. The egg out of which he emerges is the smashed world of false polarities which Sinclair, being reborn, is in the process of transcending. The bird's flying to Abraxas, or Frau Eva, respectively the symbol and the embodiment of totality, symbolizes Sinclair's ascent to the higher plane of realized Self-hood which is based, of course, on the attainment of that totality.

(b) Sinclair's relationship to the image of Frau Eva evinces a complicated dialectic process of double internalization. The initial thesis would be the original of Frau Eva in Sinclair's psyche in the form of a dream image. The subsequent antithesis would be the externalization of this image in the form of the painting. The synthesis is the later reinternalization of this projected image in the weird scene where, in a trance-like dream state, Sinclair burns the painting of Eva and eats the ashes. The image which has been completely assimilated in this way is re-externalized (new antithesis) when Sinclair meets Frau Eva in person as an empirical, external reality. She is reinternalized at the end of the book, however, (final synthesis) when the dying Demian imparts the absent Frau Eva's blessing to Sinclair in the form of a kiss. This kiss is given on the mouth, the organ of ingestion and assimilation, the same mouth that once ate the ashes of Frau Eva's picture, and thus the kiss symbolizes a reinternalization of Frau Eva's essence. Sinclair's process of self-realization is now completed.

(c) On a battlefield of World War I, Sinclair has a vision of Frau Eva that has cosmic and not just personal implications. (The empirical basis for this vision, we realize only later, is an exploding bombshell which seriously wounds Sinclair.) He describes his experience in the following way:

> In the clouds I saw a great city out
> of which millions of peoples were
> streaming forth... Into
> their midst there stepped
> a mightly, divine figure...
> with the features of Frau Eva.
> Whole processions of people
> disappeared into her, as if into
> a gigantic cave. The goddess crouched
> down on the ground... A dream
> seemed to have power over her,
> she closed her eyes and her
> great face became distorted with
> pain. Suddenly she screamed
> out loudly and out of her

> forehead stars sprang, many
> thousand shining stars which
> swung themselves into wonderful
> arches and semicircles over
> the black sky.

The meaning of this vision becomes clear if we remember that Frau Eva symbolizes the archetypal Great Mother, the origin and source of life. In going back into Frau Eva's body, mankind is returning to its origins, to the womb of humanity. The implication is, of course, not that mankind will disappear forever there, but that it will emerge reborn and renewed (the goddess's crouching position and cries of pain suggest that she is giving birth) as a higher humanity manifesting that same totality and self-realization which, with Frau Eva's help, Sinclair has already attained.

The Mark Of Cain

This symbol is introduced in **chapter two** (entitled simply "Cain") and is maintained from then until the end of the book. It is derived, of course, from the Old Testament story of Cain and Abel in Genesis, where Cain is cursed and given a mark by God because he killed Abel. Demian has a different interpretation of this story from the traditional one which Sinclair's teachers offer. According to Demian, Cain was really a superior individual, with more spirit and with more boldness and courage in his eyes, than the average man. Cain was a man with power, says Demian, whom people feared. Since there was something uncanny about him, they said he had a "mark," but the mark was really only a certain look, a certain air about him. Persons with courage and character are always uncanny, says Demian. People felt uncomfortable in the presence of a fearless and unusual person like Cain, so they invented the tale about the murder and the mark in order to get even with Cain for the fear he caused them. The mark of Cain is thus a distinguishing feature and a sign of superiority.

The point of Demian's interpretation for the novel soon becomes clear. Demian has the mark of Cain and he sees it on Sinclair. In other words, both Demian and Sinclair belong to an elite, they are among the select company of seekers of self-fulfillment about whom Hesse later wrote in "A Little Bit of Theology" that they leave the naive, child-like realm of unselfconscious innocence, incur guilt, suffer the loss of original bliss, and struggle on finally to the "third realm of the spirit" beyond good and evil, the realm of attained Self-hood. Any resemblance between these ideas about the mark of Cain as a feature of superiority, raising one above the common herd of humanity, and certain notions of Nietzsche's about the "superman" is purely intentional.

MAJOR INFLUENCES (ARRANGED ALPHABETICALLY)

Bachofen

The Swiss J. J. Bachofen (1815-1887), a jurist by training and a professor of law at the university of his native Basel by profession, is justly famous as one of the world's great pioneer historians of religion and mythology. He is credited with the discovery that prior to the paternal, patriarchal civilizations known to us from ancient history there existed all over the prehistoric Mediterranean world older and original matriarchal cultures centered around worship of the Magna Mater, the Great Mother. Obviously, Hesse's figure Frau Eva in *Demian*, with all her symbolic meaning, is influenced by Bachofen, either directly through reading Bachofen's magnum opus, *The Matriarchy* (1861), or indirectly through Jung or Dr. Lang, for Bachofen had a profound influence on Jung. There is a discussion of Bachofen's ideas in Jung's *Symbols of Transformation* which Hesse read during the *Demian* period.

The other area of Bachofen's influence on Hesse has already been referred to above (see the section on "The Bird and the Egg"). Bachofen's "Essay on the Grave Symbolism of the Ancients" (1859) discusses the idea that the black and white eggs depicted on Roman tombs represent the world with its polarities of light and darkness, death and rebirth, etc.

Bible

The language and imagery of the Bible jump at one from almost every line of *Demian*. Many turns of phrase and symbols of the novel are taken directly from the Bible. Even a quick glance at the chapter titles shows how important the Bible is for the novel: "Cain," "The Unrepentant Thief on the Cross," "Jacob's Struggle with the Angel," "Eve." We have already mentioned how closely Demian is associated with Christ (see the section "Demian" above). The course of Sinclair's life can be easily recapitulated using Biblical terminology. The "two worlds" of the first chapter can represent the traditional Christian dichotomy of good and evil. Sinclair's childhood is depicted as spent in the original paradise (the word is actually used) until he is tempted by the devil Franz Kromer (who is actually called Satan and the devil) and sins (Sinclair brags of stealing apples!) and falls from grace, only to be saved from Kromer by that Christ figure, Max Demian. For a time Sinclair attempts to return to his father in remorse and he calls himself a Prodigal Son. Ultimately Sinclair regains paradise ("goes to heaven") in the sense that at the end of the novel he has attained the chiliastic "third realm of the spirit." Sinclair's final vision of the heavenly city and of Frau Eva is based on Revelation 12: 1-2. Sinclair's dream that Demian forces him to eat the heraldic bird on the crest, after which he feels it alive within him, as well as the scene where Sinclair burns the painting of Frau Eva and eats the ashes, seems based on Revelation 10: 9-10.

German Romanticism

Ever since Hugo Ball, in his 1927 biography (see **bibliography**), called Hermann Hesse "the last knight in the glorious cavalcade of romanticism," it has been customary to view Hesse as a follower of the romantics. This view is essentially correct if one tempers it with the realization that Hesse's concern with twentieth century existential and psychological problems also makes him an author of very contemporary significance. But just what is it, nevertheless, that puts Hesse in the romantic tradition? The answer to this question can be stated simply. It is Hesse's "inwardness," his introspective emphasis on subjective, internal reality at the expense of the social milieu, his preoccupation with the inner quest for self-identity and self-realization-all aspects of which there is no lack in *Demian*.

In 1931 a collection of four of Hesse's best short stories appeared under the title The Inward Way. The title is a paraphrase of a statement found in the Fragments of the romantic poet Novalis (1772-1801): "Inwards goes the secret way," i.e. the path into the "inside," into the depths of one's soul-that is the important thing. In the introduction to the projected second part of his fragmentary main work, the novel Heinrich von Ofterdingen, Novalis writes, "Whither do we go?" and the answer he gives is "Always home." The road of life is a process of "going home," of coming to oneself, of self-realization. Novalis is explicitly named in *Demian* as being favorite reading for Emil Sinclair and there is in *Demian* even a direct quote from Heinrich von Ofterdingen: "Destiny and temperament are different names for the same concept." What links Hesse to the romantics, then, is specifically the "inward way" they both travel.

Nietzsche

It has already been mentioned in the discussion of the style of *Demian* (see "Genre, Style and Central Theme," above) that the language of *Demian* is heavily influenced by Nietzsche's *Thus Spake Zarathustra*. In 1919, the year in which *Demian* appeared, Hesse also wrote an essay entitled "Zarathustra's Return", so it is evident that Nietzsche was on Hesse's mind at the time. Nietzsche is mentioned by name twice and in a positive way by Sinclair (Nietzsche and Novalis are the only writers he cares to read), and it has already been noted in the discussion of *Demian* (see "Demian" and "The Mark of Cain," above), that the moral philosophy underlying *Demian* is essentially Nietzschean.

Some Nietzschean values to be found in *Demian* are:

1. Demian's and Sinclair's elitism, their belief in their superiority over the "herd," the "herd instinct," and the "warm nearness of the herd"' (the terms are found in *Demian* and come from *Thus Spake Zarathustra*).

2. Demian's and Sinclair's belief that it is their duty to free themselves from conventional morality in an independent search for their own values "beyond good and evil" (the term and the concept of transcending the Christian dichotomy of good and evil are both found in Nietzsche).

3. The idea that one should single-mindedly pursue one's own destiny coupled with the love of that destiny, whatever it may bring (Nietzsche referred to this love of fate with the Latin phrase amor fati).

4. Nietzsche's idea that man as we presently know him is but a transitional stage on the way to the superman, a stage to be transcended, and a stage which Zarathustra presumably has already reached. Note how Hesse uses this idea in *Demian*. Those who bear the mark of Cain are a higher species of new humanity who express nature's plan for the human race. "The will of the future is concentrated in people like us," Demian instructs Sinclair. "What nature has in store for man is written in certain individuals, in you and in me,...as it was written in Jesus and in Nietzsche."

An idea of just how close the spirit of *Demian* is to Nietzsche can be got from the following quotation from *Thus Spake Zarathustra*: "With your values and your words of good and evil you are using force, you lovers of values.... But a stronger force is emerging out of your values and a new triumph. On this the egg and the eggshell will be smashed." The image of this new power conquering the old values of good and evil as if smashing an eggshell is of course identical to Hesse's image of Sinclair's bird breaking out of the eggshell-world of false polarities.

Psychoanalysis (Freud and Jung)

No one can have read the present study up to this point and not realize that the atmosphere of depth psychology is all-pervading in *Demian*. There is, for instance, the Jungian analyst J. B. Lang, without whose influence on Hesse in 1916-1917 *Demian* would not be the novel as we know it, if it would exist at all. Dr. Lang qua Pistorius is a mouthpiece for such Jungian concepts as archetypes and the collective unconscious. As far as the other characters are concerned, Franz Kromer can be seen as an embodiment of Jung's concept of the "Shadow," Demian as the Jungian "Self," Frau Eva as "anima." In Sinclair's relationship to the Beatrice symbol we recognize Freud's concept of the "sublimation," i.e. the redirection and spiritualization of the sex drive. Sinclair's quest for self-realization can be neatly understood in terms of Jung's concept of "individuation"-according to Jung the goal of life, the realization of one's own complete and unique self-hood. This is accomplished by making conscious and developing all one's potentialities, present but latent in one's unconscious soul, a process wherein it is vital that the "Shadow" within one be accepted and integrated rather than suppressed or denied. Last not least, the whole panorama of images and symbols projected and reassimilated by Sinclair is, of course, quintessentially psychoanalytical, as is the role and function of dreams in Sinclair's life. If one were to link, for instance, Sinclair's patricidal dream in **chapter two** with his incestuous dream in **chapter five**, the result would be a classic example of Freud's Oedipus complex, as well as of his concept of dreams as symbolic wish-fulfillment. Sinclair's dreams are, of course, also Jungian in the sense that they express archetypal contents of his unconscious.

DEMIAN AS A SOCIO-POLITICAL CRITIQUE

Many of the best German novels written after World War I attempted to find rational explanations for the cataclysm of 1914-1918 (a good example is Thomas Mann's The Magic Mountain, 1924). *Demian* is such a novel. Indeed, since it was written in 1917, while the war was still raging, it has the distinction of being one of the very first of these.

Underlying the whole of *Demian* is implicit criticism of pre-1914 society as a world whose false values are based on an artificial separation of life into an officially recognized "good" half and a suppressed "bad" half. Sinclair's quest for a self-realization based on totality and the synthesis of opposites is predicated upon his existing in and breaking out of such a society. In the last two chapters of the book, however, Hesse's social criticism becomes explicit and specific. The contents of that critique will be summarized here. It encompasses both a negative criticism and a vision of hope.

HESSE'S NEGATIVE CRITICISM

1. Modern society is a compulsive, herd-like agglomeration of mutually isolated classes, each of which centripetally clings to itself out of fear and mistrust of the other ones. Hesse is not suggesting anything like the Marxist theory of class struggle here. The fear the classes have for each other is not economically based. It is psychological (or spiritual) and existential: "People flee to each other because they are afraid of each other," Demian tells Sinclair. "The upper classes form an exclusive group as do the workers and the intellectuals. And why are they afraid? One is only afraid when one is at odds with oneself. They are afraid because they have never really come to terms with their souls. We have a society composed of nothing but people who are afraid of the unknown within themselves!"

2. Something is wrong with the codes by which modern life is regulated. People are living by obsolete commandments. Religion, morality, values-all these no longer fit modern needs.

3. European civilization has become too rationalistic, materialistic, and mechanistic. "For a century or more," Demian complains, "Europe has done nothing but study and build factories. People know exactly how many grams of explosive it takes to blow up a human being, but they do not know how to pray to God; they do not even know how to amuse themselves for an hour."

4. People cling to ideals that have lost their meaning, but when someone tries to set up new ideals they stone him.

5. There will be wars and revolutions, but these will not reform the world. All they mean is that one set of owners and rulers gets exchanged for another. But nevertheless, these upheavals are not for nothing. They at least lay bare the worthlessness of contemporary values and sweep away archaic beliefs.

6. Modern society is rotten to the core and near collapse. Indeed it wishes its own downfall. On the eve of the outbreak of the war, Demian says about pre-war society: "The world as it is now constituted wants to die, it wants to perish and it will do so.... The world wants to renew itself. It smells like death. Nothing new comes without death."

HESSE'S VISION OF HOPE

It is clear from the words of Demian quoted immediately above that there is a silver lining to the dark cloud of Hesse's social criticism. The old Europe tearing itself apart, Hesse believed, was giving birth to a new humanity. This in his opinion was the real meaning of the war, and not the political and military issues conventionally associated with it: "And no matter how rigorously the world was given over to war and heroism and honor," Sinclair says, "And no matter how distant and implausible every voice of apparent humanity sounded, this was all superficial, as superficial as the question of the external and political goals of the war. In the depths something was coming into being. Something like a new humanity."

Hesse believed that the hallmark of this new humanity would be a new sense of true community based on freedom and love rather than on the fear of the old herd-like mass society. Hesse did not believe, however, that this new community could be externally induced (through political reforms, revolutions, etc.), but that it could come about only through the spontaneous mutual recognition of those lone individuals like Sinclair and Demian who (unlike the fearful masses of the herd) have come to terms with the unknown within themselves. "We who bear the mark of Cain," says Sinclair, "did not consider it our duty to worry about the shaping of the future. For us every [political] faith, every [utopian] doctrine seemed dead and useless from the start. We felt that only one thing constituted our duty and our destiny: that each one of us become totally himself and thus do complete justice to, and do the will of, nascent nature within himself, so that the uncertain future might find us ready for anything and everything, no matter what it might bring." Hesse felt strongly enough about this point to repeat it in his 1919 essay "Zarathustra's Return": "The world is not there to be reformed. Neither are you there to be reformed. You are there to be yourselves. You are there so that the world will be richer for your unique existence. If you be yourself the world will be rich and beautiful. If you do not be yourself, then the world will be poor and will seem to you to be in need of reforming."

It is through individuated, self-integrated persons like Sinclair and Demian, Hesse thought, that the will of mankind, and the will of nature, expresses itself. That is, Hesse believed that the human race was engaged in a process of spiritual evolution, and that in the likes of Demian and Sinclair the seed of man's future destiny was planted, that Demian and Sinclair were, so to speak, advanced mutations: "The will of the future is concentrated in people like us...", Demian tells Sinclair. "What nature has in store for man is written in certain individuals, in you and in me,...as it was written in Jesus and in Nietzsche."

But, it still could be asked, if this new humanity is composed of individuated persons like Demian and Sinclair who have achieved self-realization, what has that to do with the war? Demian, after all, reached his goal before the war and the fact that the final stage in Sinclair's road came in a field hospital is really accidental rather than essential. It could just as well have been in a civilian hospital in peace time, although, as we shall see presently, the symbolism of the novel would have suffered thereby. The answer to this problem is simply that Demian and, especially, Sinclair are symbols for their generation. The pain and struggle that Sinclair undergoes as an individual on the thorny path to Self-hood, Western man as a whole undergoes collectively in the suffering that is the war. The war is thus a cipher, on a universal plane, of those traumata of birth that necessarily accompany any renewal. Perhaps herein lies, in the last analysis, the secret of *Demian's* popularity. The young generation of defeated and disillusioned soldiers returning from the war did not want to feel that all the destruction, killing, and suffering were nothing more than irrational waste. Hesse gave them an opportunity to see some very flattering meaning in the hell they had just endured.

To sum up in conclusion: Hesse's social critique is not political or economical, but moral and spiritual. He did not believe that revolutions or reform schemes were an effective means of social renewal. A reborn human community of love and freedom, he was convinced, could only come about through the spiritual transformation of each individual soul.

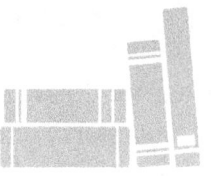

DEMIAN

INTRODUCTION

DEMIAN: THE PRODUCT OF CRISIS

It is customary to divide Hesse's career into three periods, each corresponding to a particular phase in his life:

I. 1899-1915: The Early Period (The Young Hesse)
   A. Aestheticist Trend
      1. *Romantic Songs* (1899)
      2. *An Hour Behind Midnight* (1899)
      3. *Hermann Lauscher* (1901)
   B. Realist Trend
      1. *Peter Camenzind* (1904)
      2. *Beneath the Wheel* (1906)
      3. *Rosshalde* (1914)
      4. *Knulp* (1915)

II. 1917-1932: The Middle Period (The Mature Hesse)
   A. *Demian* (1919)
   B. *Siddhartha* (1922)
   C. *Steppenwolf* (1927)

D. *Narcissus and Goldmund* (1930)
E. *Journey to the East* (1932)

III. 1933-1962: The Late Period (The Older Hesse)
A. *The Glass Bead Game* (1943)

Of supreme importance to the study of *Demian* is Hesse's passage from the Early Period to the Middle Period, a transition wrought by traumatic changes in his external circumstances and whole outlook on life. *Demian*, the product of this crisis and the record of Hesse's first therapeutic reaction to it, represents a cardinal point in Hesse's works, indeed the watershed of his career. So much is this so, that most critics date Hesse's emergence as a serious author from the appearance of this novel.

The Hesse of the early period seemed happy enough. Living successfully off his pen since 1904, he had married, had three sons, and had settled down to an idyllic life in Gaienhofen on the banks of Lake Constance. Yet beneath the surface Hesse began to grow restless: Did his retreat in Gaienhofen not represent an inability to face up to the ugly realities of modern urban life? Could the demands of home and family be reconciled with his responsibilities to himself as an artist? Or vice-versa, did not his preoccupation with artistic aesthetic matters constitute a shirking of civic and familial duty? These questions (which find expression in *Rosshalde* and *Knulp*), as well as Hesse's 1911 trip to India in search of the secret of successful communion with nature without a guilty conscience, indicate that Hesse was already at odds with his life by the end of the first period. Since he had not found peace in India, any more than he had found it in Gaienhofen, he had to conclude that the solution to his problems could not lie on the outside, in the environment, and be that environment Nature herself. Rousseau was wrong. There can be no return to nature. To attempt to do so is to indulge in infantile regression, to deny one's history and fate as a modern European man. The solution, Hesse soon saw, lay rather on the inside, in the depths of his soul. Hesse consequently gave up Gaienhofen after his return from India and went to Bern to brood. It was in this troubled state of mind that he experienced the following series of crises, the raw material for his remolding into the changed author of *Demian*:

1. World War One
   a. The magnitude of the violence, brutality and killing horrified Hesse's humane and pacifist nature.
   b. The shocked realization that if even civilized Europeans were capable of such barbarity (and even capable of glorifying it in the then-prevailing general war hysteria), then his whole optimistic concept of human nature in general and of Western civilization in particular had been superficial and false and was in dire need of radical re-evaluation.
   c. The fact that when he spoke out against the war he was excoriated and heaped with venom by his countrymen (with a concomitant loss of book sales and thus financial stability).

2. Loss of his Family
   a. The death of his father (1916)
   b. The serious illness of his youngest son (1916): cerebral meningitis
   c. The mental breakdown of his wife (1916)
   d. His divorce (1919)

Fortunately, Hesse was able to find a confidant in this time of need to whom he could turn for help. This friend was

Dr. Joseph B. Lang, a psychiatrist at the sanitarium Sonnmatt ("Sunny Meadow") in Lucerne, with whom Hesse spent more than seventy sessions in 1916-1917. Dr. Lang introduced Hesse to the psychology of C. G. Jung (especially his 1912 essay Symbols of Transformation), and this provided Hesse with the conceptual tools with which to carry out a process of therapeutic introspection that began with *Demian* and was to last, ultimately, the whole of Hesse's middle period.

PUBLISHING HISTORY OF DEMIAN

Title And Pseudonym. Although written "vehemently" in "a few fiery months" in 1917 (Hugo Ball; see **bibliography**), *Demian* was not published until 1919 when it first appeared serially in the February, March, and April numbers of *Die Neue Rundschau* (the prestigious literary periodical of Germany's then most prominent publishing house, the S. Fischer Verlag) under the title: *Demian. The History of Youth*. By Emil Sinclair. It appeared in book form a few months later under the same title and was so popular that it immediately went through eight editions! The ninth edition of 1920 (and all subsequent editions) appeared under a changed title: *Demian. The Story of Emil Sinclair's Youth*. By Hermann Hesse. In his introduction to the first American edition of *Demian* (see **bibliography**), Thomas Mann emphasized the significance of the (deliberate) ambiguity of the novel's original subtitle, The Story of Youth. This can mean, argued Mann, both the story of youth in general, or of one individual youth, Emil Sinclair, in particular. In this way, according to Mann, Hesse wished to allude to one of the novel's most important features: its universality; for Emil Sinclair is important not only as an individual, but also as the symbolic representative of a whole young generation.

It will be noted that *Demian* did not appear under Hesse's name until 1920, that before that time it appeared under the pseudonym of Emil Sinclair. Three questions suggest themselves here: (1) Why a pseudonym? (2) Why that particular pseudonym? (3) Is Hesse's use of a pseudonym unique to *Demian?*

1. Hesse had basically two interrelated reasons for using a pseudonym: (a) He had changed, he had something new and different to say in *Demian*. A new man should have a new name. The old Hesse was no longer writing, therefore the old name should not appear on the new work. (b) Hesse wanted to be read and heeded as the new man with a new message. He feared that if *Demian* were to appear under his real name, the young generation (to whom it was primarily addressed and who vehemently rejected all pre-war Impressionism in the vein of Hesse's early works) would dismiss it unread as more of the same kind of thing he had been writing in his first period.

2. Hesse experienced the first great crisis in his life at the age of thirteen when the influence of Holderlin's poetry made him decide to become a poet himself. During his second crisis, Hesse read Jung's *Symbols of Transformation* in which there is an important discussion of Holderlin. Thus this poet, whom Hesse greatly admired, has a place of sorts in the history of Hesse's development. Now one of Holderlin's greatest friends and benefactors was the German author, philosopher and courtier, Isaak von Sinclair (1775-1815). Most critics assume that Hesse had him in mind when selecting his pseudonym.

3. Hesse's use of pseudonyms is not restricted to *Demian*. One of his earliest works appeared quasi-pseudonymously as did his last work: *The Posthumous Writings and Poems*

of Hermann Lauscher. Edited by Hermann Hesse (1901), *The Glass Bead Game. The Attempt of a Life Chronicle of Magister Ludi Joseph Knecht.* Edited by Hermann Hesse (1943). This is also the case for *Steppenwolf* which pretends to be the autobiography of Harry Haller. An important essay of Hesse's appeared anonymously, if not pseudonymously, in 1919: "Zarathustra's Return". *A Word to German Youth from a German.* As far as the name Emil Sinclair is concerned, Hesse did not use this only for *Demian.* The 1919 essay "Self Reliance" appeared under this pseudonym as did the *Book of the Allemands* (1919). There are also the essays *Sinclair's Notebook*, written in 1917 but published in 1923.

The Novel's Impact. A good idea of the deep impression *Demian* made on the reading public in Germany can be had by charting the phenomenal number of editions the novel went through in rapid succession. Within a few months in 1919 eight editions had to be printed. In 1920 editions 9-26 appeared; in 1992 editions 47-56; in 1923, 57-62; in 1925, 63-65; and by 1930 the eighty-fifth edition had appeared! *Demian* was even given the Fontane Prize in 1919, a literary award for first novels of promising young writers. But since "Emil Sinclair" was not really such an author, Hesse returned the prize.

When *Demian* first appeared, Thomas Mann wrote the publisher (also his publisher), S. Fischer, extolling the novel and asking urgently, "Tell me please, who is Emil Sinclair? How old is he? Where does he live? His *Demian*...has made a bigger impression on me than any new work has for a long time." Fischer answered that he did not know, that Hermann Hesse had sent in the manuscript on the behalf of Sinclair. The secret could not be kept. Critics soon began to suspect that Sinclair was really Hesse, so in the July, 1920 issue of the magazine Vivos Voco, of which he was co-editor, Hesse admitted the truth. Henceforth the novel would appear under its changed title.

In his introduction to the first American edition of *Demian*, Thomas Mann compares the wildfire spread of the novel's fame to one of the greatest literary sensations of Europe, the appearance of Goethe's *The Sorrows of Young Werther* in 1774. "Unforgettable," writes Mann, "is the electrifying effect which was caused immediately after the [First] World War by the *Demian* of a certain mysterious Sinclair. This was a work which touched the nerve of the times, and which enthralled a whole young generation is thankful bliss, a generation which thought that out of their midst had arisen the prophet of their deepest Selves (while in reality it was a forty-two-year-old who gave them what they needed)... One should think of Werther, of whom the impact of *Demian* in Germany reminds one to a certain degree."

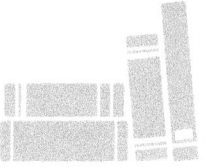

DEMIAN

TEXTUAL ANALYSIS

CHAPTER ONE: TWO WORLDS

> MOTTO

"All I wanted to do was to try to live what wanted to express itself in me anyway. Why was that so terribly difficult?"

    This motto is taken from **chapter five** and is spoken by Sinclair at that critical point in his life, just before he meets Pistorius, when he is alone at boarding school and strange symbolic images and dreams are welling up within him. The motto expresses the central theme of the novel in a nutshell: The story of Sinclair's life is the story of his search for himself, for self-identity. This, in turn, is seen in terms of entelechy, that is, the attainment of selfhood is, ultimately, a process of realizing those potentialities which exist in one as latent, unconscious qualities-latent but not passive. They have a dynamism of their own, autonomous of the conscious ego, and one ignores them at one's peril. Strangely, the search for self-identity proves to be one of the most difficult tasks one can undertake in life, which explains why most of mankind would prefer to vegetate. Sinclair, however, is a superior individual who is willing to try to live what wants to express itself in him.

PROLOGUE

The prologue stands within the fictional framework of the novel, not outside it. It is written (like the rest of the book) in the first person by Emil Sinclair as an introduction to the methodology and themes, of this, his autobiography.

Methodology

Sinclair begins with some very important points as to the manner in which his story is written. It is not a novel, he says. There is no omniscient narrator hovering God-like over the hero to relate objectively all there is to know about him, nor is the hero of Sinclair's story a fictitious character. The chapters following the prologue are, he says, the story of a real, unique, flesh-and-blood human being: Sinclair himself. We are to be given the story of Sinclair's life as he lived it, and not as someone else would have seen it. We are dealing, thus, with what purports to be a highly subjective and personal type of intimate autobiography that makes no apologies for its subjectivity.

Themes

Some of the major themes of the book are touched upon briefly in the prologue. These can be summarized in short as follows:

1. Each individual is absolutely unique. Everyone must find his own way in life, define for himself his own goals. "We

can understand each other, but each individual can only be his own interpreter."

2. The life of every person is a thorny way to himself. No one has ever been completely himself, but all strive to attain selfhood, some dully, some more easily-each as best he can.

3. Sinclair is not a sage but a seeker. He no longer looks to the stars or in books, however, for answers to the riddle of life, but into himself, so that he can, as he puts it, "begin to hear the teachings of my blood rushing within me."

4. Human evolution is not yet completed. Every individual is "a cast of nature's die in the direction of [ultimate] humanity." Some have progressed further than others towards the final goal, but we all have the same origin: "the mothers," i.e. the maternal principle, the fundamental matrix of life common to all men.

TITLE

The title refers to a fundamental aspect of the central theme of the novel: The problem of polarity or dualism in the civilization of the modern West, split up into a world of "light" and a world of "darkness." The novel begins, significantly, with Sinclair's first becoming aware of this basic dualism at the age of ten. The specific form the polarity takes in **chapter one** lies in the sharp contrast Sinclair sees between the clean, proper, pious, well-ordered and virtuous home of his parents with its (upper) middle-class values on the one hand, and the lower-class world of servant girls and apprentices, of drunkenness, vice, superstition, violence, scandal, and crime on the other. Sinclair is amazed at how close together these two worlds exist, side by side, and at how easy it is to move from one world to the other, as in the case of the family maid, Lina. But yet, in spite of the close proximity, there is a fundamental dichotomy: "Two worlds were intermingled there [i.e. in Sinclair's home town], from two poles came day and night."

Purpose Of Chapter One

Chapter one shows how the crucial first step in Sinclair's journey to himself is accomplished by his being wrenched out of his childhood innocence and the spiritual shelter of his parental home through his encounter with Franz Kromer and the "dark" world he represents. Painful though it may be, this process is necessary: "Everyone," says Sinclair, "must have destroyed the pillars of his childhood before he can become himself." According to Hesse there simply cannot be any spiritual growth without coming to terms with the sin, pain, and suffering that a sojourn in the "dark" world necessarily entails, without a kind of death. Sinclair the innocent child must "die" so that a new, guilty but more mature Sinclair might live. The metaphor of death and rebirth used here to describe the first step in Sinclair's spiritual growth is picked up again by Hesse in the last chapter to symbolize the emergence of a new humanity in World War I.

Biblical Symbolism

Sinclair's loss of childhood innocence is depicted by the use of Biblical imagery. The "light" world of his parents is called a "paradise" (replete with Sinclair's ethereal sisters in their long white gowns who remind one of angels), his encounter with Kromer a "fall from paradise. "Sinclair's original sin is, appropriately, the boastful fabrication that he stole apples. Kromer is specifically referred to several times as the devil or as "the Enemy," a common euphemism for the devil (German der Feind, related to English the fiend). Sinclair wishes fervently that he could play the Prodigal Son and overcome his difficulties by simply confessing to his parents, but for the time being he cannot bring himself to do so.

Jungian Symbolism

In his function as the living antithesis of everything Sinclair's parental world of "light" stands for, Kromer can be seen as an embodiment of the Jungian "Shadow," the "dark" or "bad" side of the psyche. Hesse hints at this when Sinclair describes the termination of one of his meetings with Kromer: "He cast a terrible glance into my eyes, spit once more, and disappeared like a shadow" (Italics added). Sinclair feels defiled by this meeting.

Sinclair And The "Dark" World

We have already seen how amazed Sinclair was that the "two worlds" should exist so close to one another, in spite of their opposite natures. Just how close we soon find out when Sinclair begins to suspect dimly that the "dark" and "light" worlds actually co-exist within him as parts of his soul. That there is something of Franz Kromer in Sinclair is indicated right at the beginning of the chapter when he calls the "dark" side "enticing," and a little later when Sinclair relates that when stories of prodigal sons were read at home, he found himself, in spite of himself, liking the part of the story depicting the sons' profligacy better than the part where they reformed and came home. About this secret identification with the "dark" side of life, Sinclair says, "It was simply there somehow as an inkling, a possibility, down deep in my emotions." This feeling that the dark world may be part of himself is also expressed obliquely in the series of rhetorical questions through which Sinclair realizes his complicity in his "fall from paradise."

Once Sinclair fully realizes (in **chapter three**) that the "Shadow" is present not only in Franz Kromer, but also as part of himself, he will have taken a major stride on his way to himself. The beginnings of this realization, depicted in **chapter one**, are an important part of the initial progress towards Sinclair's goal that is the topic of this chapter.

Dreams

Dreams form an important part of *Demian*. They accompany every stage in Sinclair's development. Thus it is not surprising that, in the form of nightmares Sinclair has about Kromer, the dream motif should be introduced in the first chapter.

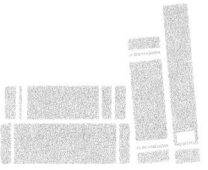

DEMIAN

TEXTUAL ANALYSIS

CHAPTER TWO: CAIN

| TITLE

The title refers to the Cain who killed Abel. The Old Testament brothers function in this chapter as symbols of Sinclair's varying states of mind. Cain and Abel, as Sinclair only dimly understands Demian's unorthodox interpretation of the Biblical story, come to symbolize for him the "dark" and the "light" worlds respectively. As Sinclair pendulates in this chapter between these two worlds, he identifies now with Cain, now with Abel.

| **Purpose of Chapter Two**

1. This chapter introduces Demian and establishes his function as Sinclair's mentor. 2. The next steps in Sinclair's development are shown as he pendulates for the first time between the "light" and the "dark" worlds. The world of Sinclair's childhood receives further blows. 3. The bird on the crest over the portal of

Sinclair's home is introduced. This will, of course, figure later in the novel as the important symbol of the bird breaking out of the world-egg. 4. The idea of the mark of Cain is introduced as the distinguishing sign of a spiritual elite of courageous individuals embarked on the journey to self-realization.

Sinclair's Development

It is during Demian's very first conversation with Sinclair that Demian tells him his novel interpretation of the story of Cain and Abel (see "The Mark of Cain," Chapter III, above). Later Sinclair compares the traditional view of the story with Demian's version and applies the conclusions to himself. From the conventional point of view, he says, he had been a "kind of Abel" living in a "world of purity and light." But now he had, like Cain, sunk deep into a different fallen world. But, Sinclair soon realizes, the situation is not as simple as that. There is something to Demian's view, too, for had not he, Sinclair, felt superior to his father, felt contempt for him and his world of light? Had he not believed he could see through his father because he had a secret from him and knew of things of which his father's world had no conception? Now he was Demian's Cain, the proud Cain for whom the "mark" was a distinction. And was not Demian, too, a kind of Cain in this sense? Sinclair's positive identification with Cain is completed in a dream in which he attempts to murder his father. Sinclair has symbolically recapitulated Cain's crime.

If Sinclair began to realize dimly in **chapter one** that the "Shadow" was part of his soul, he is beginning now, in seeing himself as the proud Cain, to take the very important initial steps in integrating the dark side of his nature into the total psyche.

The next step in Sinclair's way to himself has begun: "A stone had fallen into the well, and the well was my young soul. And for a long, a very long time this matter with Cain, the murder [he means both the fratricide in the story and his patricidal dream] and the mark was the point at which my attempts at insight, doubt and criticism took their start."

Sinclair is, of course, still a long way from the ultimate synthesis of the Cain and Abel within him. He is still in a disequilibrium state of pendulation between the two worlds. Hardly has be begun to accept his "Shadow" when he utterly rejects it again, wishing to return completely to the lost innocence of the world of "light." The only thing standing in the way of Sinclair's return is his subjection to Kromer, but this obstacle is soon removed by Demian's intervention, after which Kromer actually becomes afraid of Sinclair and avoids him at all costs.

Sinclair confesses everything about his lies and stealing to his parents and returns to the world of his childhood. Once he is re-established in "paradise," Sinclair sets about to forget Kromer, and even Demian too: "[Demian], too, was a tempter, he, too, bound me to the other, the evil, bad world, and I wanted to forget that world forever. I could not and did not want to give up Abel and help to glorify Cain, now when I had just become Abel again." Happy as he is in the new-found peace of childhood innocence, Sinclair realizes inwardly that all is not really in order. His return has something of infantile regression about it. Sinclair realizes that he is not yet an independent person able to stand on his own two feet. From original dependence on his parents, he fell under Kromer's control, only to be released by Demian, and not by himself. Now he had returned home again and was once more dependent upon his parents.

Biblical Symbolism

Sinclair speaks of the world as a "vale of tears," of his association with Kromer as a "damnation." He speaks of the loss and regain of "paradise." Fittingly, Sinclair also calls Demian's intervention on his behalf a "salvation." Kromer, who was called the devil in **chapter one**, is called "Satan" several times in this chapter. Finally, Sinclair calls his return to his parents the "return of the Prodigal Son." It does not need to be mentioned, of course, that Cain and Abel figure prominently in this chapter.

Jungian Symbolism

Kromer's status as a symbol of the Jungian "Shadow" is quite clearly alluded to in a statement of Sinclair's: "In my dreams [Kromer] lived with me as my shadow...." Demian's status as a symbol of Jung's concept of the "Self" (see "Demian" in Chapter III, above) is alluded to when Sinclair comments: "As if in a dream I was subject to [Demian's] voice, his influence.... Wasn't that a voice that could only come out of myself?" This statement will be repeated almost verbatim in **chapter four**, but then, in order to make the identification between Demian and Sinclair's "Self" closer, Sinclair's words are spoken by Demian. It is worth noting that Kromer and Demian in their symbolic function as "Shadow" and "Self" respectively, are, in the above quotations, associated with dreams. According to Jung the "Shadow" and the "Self" are archetypes of the collective unconscious, and dreams are, Jung says, one of the primary voices of these archetypes.

Dreams

In this chapter the dream motif introduced in **chapter one** functions prominently. We have already mentioned Sinclair's patricidal dream. Another very significant dream is the one in which Sinclair dreams Kromer is kneeling on him. But then the figure changes, and it is Demian who is kneeling on Sinclair. The significance of this dream is that the place Kromer occupied in Sinclair's life is being taken by Demian. In Jungian terms one could say that the "Self" is beginning to replace the "Shadow's" leading role in Sinclair's psyche. The dream is thus an indication of Sinclair's progress towards self-realization.

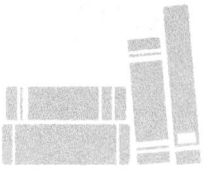

DEMIAN

TEXTUAL ANALYSIS

CHAPTER THREE: THE THIEF UPON THE CROSS

TITLE

The title refers to the unrepentant thief crucified next to Christ. During confirmation class Demain tells Sinclair that contrary to the Biblical interpretation, it is the unrepentant, not the repentant thief who deserves our respect. In not breaking down at the last moment and asking Christ's blessing he remained true to himself to the end and manifested great strength of character. The connection between this reinterpretation of the bad thief and Demian's version of the Cain and Abel story is obvious.

Just as the re-evaluation of Cain started Sinclair on some very important thinking about himself, so too, the new view of the bad thief represents a milestone in Sinclair's further development, but not only for what it represents in itself ("Be strong; be true to yourself"), but in that it initiates a very important theological conversation between Demian and Sinclair which leads Sinclair to valuable new insights about himself.

Sinclair's Development

After returning to the "light" world of his parents, Sinclair lived "beautiful, tender and lovely" years of childhood, "sheltered by father and mother, [and] by filial love..."until, as he says, "the world of my childhood fell apart." The cause of this ruination was the onset of puberty. Sexual awakening seemed to Sinclair as "an enemy, a destroyer,...temptation and sin." It is not long before Sinclair draws the obvious conclusions about his new state: "What once had been Franz Kromer, that existed now within myself." In other words, the important realization, implicit in chapters one and two, that the "Shadow" is actually part of himself and not only external, has fully and explicitly dawned on Sinclair. But this is not all. He has gained a further insight as well. If the "dark" world is in him and not "out there," then there can be no escape from it, for one cannot escape from oneself. Therefore his attempt to re-enter the "light" world of original bliss had been wrong. Sinclair now realizes that one can never go back. To try to do so would be to arrest one's development, to commit a grave crime against one's sacred duty to self-fulfillment (hence the adjective "murderous"). These insights represent key stages in Sinclair's inward journey to himself. They are soon to be followed by other important ones imparted by Demian.

After he has told Sinclair his views on the bad thief (see "Title," above), Demian goes on, relating now his view that the Judeo-Christian concept of God is one-sided, representing only qualities of goodness, nobility, fatherly love, etc. But the world, says Demian, does not only consist of such qualities, and so everything else is simply ascribed to the devil. One half of reality is suppressed and ignored. It makes no sense, he continues, to call God the father of all life while at the same time repressing sexuality, upon which, after all, life is based, or calling sex sinful and the work of the devil. There should be a god who encompasses the devil within himself and before whom one does not have to shut one's eyes when the most natural things in the world happen, Demian concludes. (We learn in **chapter five** that this god is, of course, Abraxas.)

It now dawns on Sinclair that Demian's words about God and the devil correspond exactly to his own ideas about the "two worlds of 'light' and 'darkness'." This means that what he had thought was a private notion, of concern only to himself and his own personal development, was in fact part of "the universal stream of great ideas." Sinclair sees this as meaning that the problems of his development have universal human significance, that what is happening to him is important not only for himself as an individual, but for the whole human race. When Sinclair then tells Demian of his theory of the "two worlds," Demian realizes that Sinclair has put his finger on one of the fundamental truths of life, but also that he is, as yet, not advanced enough to encompass the two poles in a synthesis-the ultimate goal of life. It should be noted here how Demian talks in terms of a dualism of thought and life, and how he pleads for a union of these opposites.

The conversation then turns to the question of morality. Demian says that since there is no such thing as an absolute or universal moral code (a glance at history and comparative ethnology tells him this), it is up to each individual to decide for himself what is forbidden and what is allowed. To blindly follow conventional morality as most do, Demian says, is a sign of laziness. Here too, Sinclair has not yet progressed far enough (nor can he yet be expected to) to have evolved for himself his own standards of conduct.

Demian

Most of the essential features of Demian as a symbol of totality (see "Demian," Chapter III, above), are presented to the reader in this chapter. There is also a strong hint, presented here, that Demian may live in an incestuous relationship with his mother (on the significance of the incest motif, see "Frau Eva," Chapter III, above). Demian's role as Sinclair's mentor is superbly demonstrated during the confirmation classes he and Sinclair attend together. The purpose of the minister's instruction is to prepare the boys for their initiation into the mysteries of the Christian religion. For Sinclair, however, the significant thing was that during this period he was initiated by Demian, instead, into the mysteries of life. In other words, Hesse uses the framework of a confirmation class to show how important Demian's role as spiritual guide is for Sinclair. Demian assumes in Sinclair's life the role the church and her teachings would normally take.

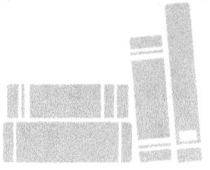

DEMIAN

TEXTUAL ANALYSIS

CHAPTER FOUR: BEATRICE

TITLE

Beatrice, the "heavenly, beloved one" in the Divine Comedy, has been since Dante's time a symbol of spiritual purity. Sinclair gives this name to a beautiful girl he sees in a park (he never meets or talks to her) because she is for him an embodiment of just that purity which, during this his time of dissipation, he most lacks and therefore most longs for. The encounter with Beatrice is a crucial one for Sinclair, for because of it his search for himself takes on a new intensity (see discussion of Beatrice in "Background to Demian").

Sinclair's Development

Sinclair's childhood world collapsed without there being anything positive to take its place. In this vulnerable state he falls all too easily under the bad influence of an experienced older boy, Alfons Beck, who initiates him in debauchery. In this spiritual vacuum, which Sinclair calls "a strange emptiness and isolation," and afraid of his new feelings towards the opposite sex, Sinclair is driven to seek escape among a group of carousing young rowdies.

Sinclair has fallen from the one extreme of the frenetic innocence of his post-Kromer return to childhood to the other extreme of wanton drunkenness. He realizes that he has pendulated once again from the world of "light" to the "dark" world. Sinclair suffers just as much now as he once did under Franz Kromer's thumb. It is in this state of mind that he encounters Beatrice and sees in her the symbol of purity, the ideal, he needs to help him overcome his fall. Under the influence of Beatrice, Sinclair turns completely from vice to virtue, he even sublimates his sexual desire.

Sinclair has now retreated, once again, to the world of "light," but this time, as he realizes, there is a significant difference. This time the element of infantile regression is missing: "the present 'world of light' was more or less my own creation; it was no longer...a sanctuary without duties; it was a new service I invented and demanded of myself, with responsibilities and self-discipline." In trying to express his new disposition Sinclair turns to painting. At first he tries to paint Beatrice, but when that does not succeed he goes over to free creation, simply painting any face, following his imagination. What eventually emerges is a portrait of Demian, a painting that has a profound effect on Sinclair; he even dreams of it several times. Later he paints the picture of the bird breaking out of the world-egg and sends it to Demian. By this time he has completely forgotten Beatrice and is now under the spell of his paintings of Demian and the bird.

Painting Of Demian

The painting's mode of origin throws important light on its meaning. Sinclair tells how it came into being: "Finally I finished a face one day - I was almost unconscious - that spoke to me more strongly than all the previous ones." We have here a perfect description of psychic projection (on projection, see "Beatrice" in Chapter III, above). What Sinclair puts on canvas is a direct expression, a "projection," of his unconscious. His painting is a symbol of the Self (Symbol is meant here in its deep, Jungian sense of "icon," epiphany, manifestation, disclosure. On the Self, see the discussion of Demian in Chapter III, above.) As a projected symbol of the Self, the painting is a portrait of Demian who functions in the novel as the embodiment of the Self per se. But, as we shall see, the painting is also identical with Sinclair whose own individual Self the picture represents as well.

The painting's mode of origin indicated that it is a psychic projection. That the contents of that projection constitute a symbol of the Self, however, is indicated, as we saw, by its being a portrait of Demian, and more importantly, as we shall see, by what Sinclair says about it - words which can only refer to the Self, Sinclair's personal Self: "Gradually a feeling came over me that [the picture] was not Beatrice and not Demian but - myself. The picture did not look like me - it wasn't supposed to I felt - but it was the essence which constituted my life, it was my innermost soul, my fate or my guiding spirit [Damon]..." It should be noted here that this painting, important as it is, is only a first step. It is followed by an even more important one in **chapter six**: Sinclair's portrait of a face which unites the features of Demian and Frau Eva.

> "Destiny And Temperament Are Names Of The Same Concept."

This aphorism, taken from the German romantic poet Novalis (1772-1801), Sinclair puts at the bottom of his painting as its motto. The motto is thus a kind of interpretation of the painting and Sinclair's new understanding of the maxim's meaning throws light on the stage his development has reached at this point in his life.

Briefly, what Novalis seems to be saying is that one's destiny is something that already exists in a hidden and latent form deep inside of one. No facet of life which impinges upon one from the outside can have ultimate significance in terms of one's final destiny unless it corresponds to what is in one to begin with, so that one's life is a process of expression as much as impression, or, to put it the other way round, not only is external fate an expression of our inner being, but, conversely, one should be so fully at one with oneself, that anything that happens to one as a result of an external force is totally assimilated and made an integral part of one's own being. Only in this way is one free, for only then is that which must be (fate, destiny) identical to that which one wants to be (one's will, one's self expressing itself). This is, of course, very close to the Nietzschean amor fati (see discussion of Nietzsche in "Background to Demian"), i.e. love of fate, the perfect coincidence of external exigency and internal drive. The fact that, in encountering the self-projected symbol of his Self, Sinclair now understands the meaning of the maxim, means that he has become aware of the existence of this inner drive and has realized that his destiny is self-realization, which can come about only by developing his innermost essence (i.e. entelechy, see p. 4, above), and not by conformity to external values, such as those of his father's "light" world, for instance. This is an important step indeed in Sinclair's way to himself.

It should be noted in conclusion that Novalis' aphorism is difficult to translate. The word rendered above as "temperament" is Gemut in the original German, a word with no exact English equivalent. It means all at once "mind," "heart," "soul," "spirit," "feeling," "temperament," "emotion," "disposition," "sensitivity." Perhaps if one realizes this, the interpretation of the motto offered here will seem clearer.

Dreams

Sinclair reports that it was during this period of his life, described in **chapter four**, that he began to dream frequently again, seemingly after a pause of several years. His dreams contain various symbols from his unconscious which he describes as "new kinds of images" and they include frequent dreams of his portrait of Demian which came alive and talked to him. As a matter of fact, it is only after one such dream that Sinclair realizes that the face in the painting is Demian's. The most important dream in this chapter is not about the portrait, however, but about the other picture, of the heraldic bird. Sinclair dreams that Demian is holding the bird in his hands, that it comes alive, and that Demian then forces him to eat it, whereupon the bird begins to fill up Sinclair's insides and to consume him. He then wakes up, "full of the fear of death." What does this strange dream mean?

The bird is an archetypal symbol of the soul, here Sinclair's soul (see "The Bird and the Egg," Chapter III, above). As such it is, like the Demian portrait, a projected symbol of Sinclair's Self. When Demian, Sinclair's spiritual guide, makes Sinclair eat the bird, Sinclair is, in effect, reassimilating the projected image of his soul, he is integrating his psyche by appropriating his Self to himself. We know enough about Hesse's interpretation of death as the prelude to rebirth on a higher plane to know why Sinclair should wake up "full of the fear of death." The old, childish Sinclair, who pendulated dependently between the "light" and "dark" worlds, is dying, and the new, more mature Sinclair is being born.

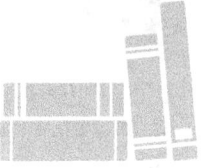

DEMIAN

TEXTUAL ANALYSIS

CHAPTER FIVE: THE BIRD STRUGGLES OUT OF THE EGG

....

| TITLE

The title refers to the interpretation Demian gives to Sinclair's painting, but, on a deeper level, also to Sinclair himself. Sinclair sent his painting of the heraldic bird in the crest over the portal of his father's house to Demian and received a cryptic answer. As we have seen (see "The Bird and the Egg," in "Background to Demian"), the bird represents Sinclair, or his soul, in the struggle to overcome the "light"/"dark" world of false polarities by breaking out of that world and flying to Abraxas, the god who symbolizes totality, the union of opposites. The death-rebirth motif is also included in Demian's message. For Sinclair to grow ("be born," as Demian puts it), he must destroy his old world (death), but the fact that that world is depicted as an egg out of which a bird is emerging suggests, of course, rebirth. The title, the picture, Demian's message - these all capture symbolically the essence of Sinclair's development towards self-realization which is seen, ultimately, as the attainment of totality, of integration of all opposites in the psyche and in the world.

Purpose Of Chapter Five

This is a short, transitional chapter serving the following important functions: 1. The Abraxas symbol is introduced along with the idea the god represents, namely the union of opposites or synthesis of polarities. 2. Pistorius is introduced and the first part of his lesson for Sinclair is imparted to him. 3. The next steps in Sinclair's development (partly induced by Pistorius) are depicted.

Sinclair's Development

With the help of the Beatrice symbol, Sinclair was able, for a time, to sublimate his sex drive. But as we have seen above, Beatrice's place in Sinclair's soul is soon taken by his paintings of Demian and the bird. Beatrice no longer suffices Sinclair. Once more the sex drive emerges, demanding other images and goals than those represented by Beatrice. But by this time, due to the influence of his Demian portrait, Sinclair has reached a new, higher plane of development. He no longer pendulates from the "light" to the "dark" world and back again. He is interested now in the synthesis of those opposites, not an oscillation between them. Thus Sinclair does not go from the pure, Platonic spirituality of Beatrice to the opposite extreme of base lust. Instead, he feels a deep longing for someone in whom a kind of love can be consummated that unites the poles of spirituality and sensuality, that synthesizes all opposites. At this stage Sinclair has already encountered the symbol of this love in Abraxas. Later he will come to know its living embodiment: Frau Eva.

The experience of this new kind of love is but one of Sinclair's advancements in this chapter. Through his friendship with Pistorius he learns that his dreams and feelings arising from that love are of an archetypal nature, or, as Pistorius tells Sinclair in summing up this important lesson, "And now you can see how little your soul is 'personal' in its depths." Through Pistorius, in other words, Sinclair comes to the appreciation that within him there dwells a whole vast realm that is the richness of the collective unconscious. Without this insight, self-realization (i.e. the conscious integration of the archetypes of the collective unconscious) is impossible.

Dreams

It is in this chapter that Sinclair has the most important dream of his life. It is the incestuous dream in which he is embracing his mother, but in which, as he does so, the figure changes into another as yet unknown woman with whom he exchanges an intensely erotic embrace. Only later will Sinclair learn that that woman is Frau Eva. Spell-bound, Sinclair continues to dream of this strange, enchanting woman, whom he now identifies with Abraxas, and who, he now knows, is the ultimate desired object of this new love of his which unites opposites.

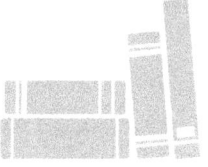

DEMIAN

TEXTUAL ANALYSIS

CHAPTER SIX: JACOB'S STRUGGLE

> **TITLE**

The title is taken from the Jacob in the Old Testament who was blessed because he wrestled with God (or the angel of God) and won (Genesis 32, 24-30). It refers here, however, to Sinclair in his struggle with the images projected from his unconscious psyche (in this chapter chiefly Sinclair's painting of his dream vision of Frau Eva). The title also refers to Sinclair's successful struggle to overcome his growing dependence upon Pistorius about whom he says significantly in this context: "Out of his mouth God had spoken to me." In the Bible Jacob, though victorious, was wounded by the angel. In *Demian* the "wound" Sinclair receives is simply that, necessary as it is to outgrow Pistorius and become independent of him, it nevertheless hurts Sinclair to have to inwardly distance himself from his friend. Sinclair even feels that in turning away from Pistorius who had given him so much (but who had no more to give him) he is committing a kind of crime against this, his spiritual brother."...for the first time I felt the mark of Cain on my brow," Sinclair says after his break with Pistorius. The mark of Cain as Jacob's wound-in this unique way Hesse has blended two Biblical images to symbolize Sinclair's situation.

The Picture Of Frau Eva

It is in this chapter that Sinclair's last and ultimate psychic projection takes place in the form of his painting of the mysterious woman in his dreams, a face which, as Sinclair later learns, is that of Frau Eva herself. At first Sinclair merely dreams of her and imagines her in his daydreams. His attempts to paint her fail. But at last he succeeds, creating a portrait "smeared on canvas as if unconscious." (In Sinclair's description of this painting process we recognize, of course, the same unconscious projection we witnessed in the earlier painting of Demian.) There can be no doubt that this picture, even more so than the earlier one of Demian, is a symbol of the Self, of Sinclair's Self. As with the picture of Demian, Sinclair's comments on the Frau Eva image indicate this.

We have already seen in the discussion of **chapter four** how Sinclair integrated an earlier projected symbol of his Self (the picture of the heraldic bird) by dreaming that Demian made him eat it. The act of ingestion as a symbol of the re-appropriation of the Self to oneself is repeated in this chapter, but with the significant difference that now no one is standing over Sinclair forcing him to eat. The eating is done of his own volition. Sinclair reports that, either in a dream or in a trance-like reality (he is not sure which), he burned the painting of Frau Eva and consumed the ashes.

In what sense is the image of Frau Eva a more important projection, a better symbol of the Self, than the earlier painting of Demian? The first and most obvious answer would be that although Frau Eva, as a symbol of totality, evinces strikingly androgynous features, she is, nevertheless, a woman. Thus when Sinclair, as a man, projects and reassimilates a symbol of his Self in the form of an image of Frau Eva, a woman, the idea of totality, of the synthesis of opposites, is better expressed than it was in the case of Demian's image. Jung says that in the psyche of every man there exists a female principle which he called the "anima." (In the female psyche, conversely, there is a male principle, the "animus.") Now self-realization or psychic integration is based, as we have seen, on the union of opposites. Thus every man must come to terms with the female side of his nature, his "anima" (and, of course, every woman with her "animus"). In seeing in Frau Eva the symbol of his Self, and in becoming one with that symbol by eating the ashes of her burnt image, Sinclair has, in effect, integrated his "anima" and has thereby achieved a higher stage of psychic synthesis.

A second answer to the question posed above would be that Frau Eva is more intimately connected with Sinclair's existential problems than is Demian. To be sure, Demian is Sinclair's friend and spiritual guide, but Frau Eva is the object of that new kind of love which overwhelmed him after the Beatrice episode. Frau Eva, that is, is at the center of that whole complexly interwoven web of Sinclair's sexuality, spirituality, identity and fate.

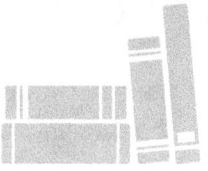

DEMIAN

TEXTUAL ANALYSIS

CHAPTERS SEVEN AND EIGHT: FRAU EVA; THE BEGINNING OF THE END

By the end of **chapter six**, Sinclair's development is essentially completed. The remaining two chapters serve only to add the final touches confirming his achievement of self-realization and to show the transpersonal significance of Sinclair's story by projecting the key symbols connected with his development and fate (namely the heraldic bird and Frau Eva) onto the broad, universal screen that is World War I. It is in chapter seven that Sinclair sees the vision in the thunder clouds of his bird breaking out of its world-egg-a harbinger of the war, and in chapter eight that his vision of Frau Eva occurs as a kind of universal Great Mother emerging out of the chaos of the war to give birth to a new humanity.

The final touches to Sinclair's development in the last two chapters can be dealt with briefly. Having finally met Frau Eva in person in chapter seven, Sinclair realizes that he has come to an important juncture in his life. "I had arrived at a high point in the road," he says, "from where I could see the further path, broad and magnificent, striving towards lands of promise." It is clear from Sinclair's use of this road metaphor to describe his encounter with Frau Eva that she represents, in the last analysis, but a station on Sinclair's journey to himself, albeit the most important or highest one. (Notice too how Sinclair says "a goal" in the quotation above and not "the goal."). Just as Sinclair had to outgrow Beatrice and become independent of Pistorius, so, too, he must not lean on Frau Eva, for there can be no self-realization without self-reliance. Frau Eva realizes this herself when she talks with Sinclair in chapter seven about his relationship to her. However, there are various ways of not being dependent on another person. In the case of so important a figure as Frau Eva there can be no question of Sinclair's putting her behind himself as he did with Beatrice and Pistorius. The answer lies here in becoming independent of the empirical person Frau Eva by internalizing her essence. This process, begun when Sinclair ate the ashes of her image in **chapter six**, is continued in chapter seven and finished in chapter eight, at the end of the novel, when Demian imparts to Sinclair Frau Eva's kiss.

As for the titles of the last two chapters, they are more or less self-explanatory. "Frau Eva" is put at the head of chapter seven because it is here that she enters the novel in person and here that Sinclair meets her for the first time. Chapter eight is called "The Beginning of the End" because it marks the outbreak of World War I, the beginning of the end of the old, pre-war world with its false values. The title also refers to the beginning of the end of Sinclair's search for himself, a quest whose completion is noted at the very end of the book when Sinclair realizes that now, at last, he is like Demian who was his friend and guide.

In conclusion it should be noted that almost all of the explicit social and political criticism of the novel occurs in the last two chapters, especially in chapter seven (see "*Demian* as a Socio-Political Critique.")

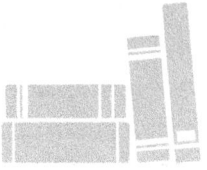

DEMIAN

DEMIAN AND THE CRITICS

The significant criticism on *Demian* begins, oddly enough, only after World War II, in spite of the novel's great popularity throughout the 1920's and early 30's. A glance at the following dates indicates how recent the major criticism is: Matzig's book, *Hermann Hesse in Montagnola*, with its important chapter on *Demian*, appeared in 1947, and Seidlin's article on the novel, "The Exorcism of the Demon," in 1950. Not until eight years later, in 1958, do we have Dahrendorf's article on *Demian* and Jungian psychology. Then there is another pause until 1965, the year in which Rose's and Ziolkowski's books on Hesse appeared, each containing long chapters on *Demian*. 1967 saw the appearance of Boulby's book on Hesse's prose which also, of course, devotes a chapter to *Demian*. In 1968 Neumann's long article, "Hermann Hesses *Demian*-eine Analyse," was published. In 1970, finally, Field's book on Hesse, replete with its chapter on *Demian*, appeared in the Twayne series on modern authors. It should be noted, too, that with the exception of Dahrendorf, Matzig and Neumann, all these critics are writing primarily for a North American public. Boulby is a British citizen teaching in Canada. Field is a Canadian, and Rose, Seidlin and Ziolkowski are Americans. This is further indication that Hesse is currently more popular here than in Europe.

Demian is not a bone of contention among the critics. There has always been a consensus about what the major theme of the novel is: *Demian* is seen as basically a Bildungsroman in the romantic tradition, but updated by the use of twentieth-century psychoanalytical and existential motifs, and by dealing with broad contemporary issues about the relation of the individual to modern society, a Bildungsroman which tells of Emil Sinclair's search for himself.

Critics have emphasized different aspects of Sinclair's search. Matzig points to the mythological and anthropological background to the novel, which stems from Bachofen; Frau Eva as a symbol of the Great Mother is, of course, important here. Seidlin objects to the overemphasis he feels some critics have put on the Freudian and Jungian aspects of *Demian* and emphasizes more the spiritual and existential sides of Sinclair's quest. Dahrendorf, on the other hand, is able to show just how much of C. G. Jung's theories there is in the novel. Rose throws light on the ways in which *Demian* is at one and the same time firmly planted in the German romantic tradition and yet not a derivative or imitative work, but a thoroughly modern novel-as its contemporary impact indeed confirms. Yet this synthesis of tradition and modernity is no mean achievement on Hesse's part. Ziolkowski points to the Nietzschean, Biblical and existential influences that figure in Hesse's novel; he shows how these sources are skillfully woven into the very structural fabric of the novel rather than being merely artificially "pasted on" as it were. Most critics have always assumed that with *Demian*, Hesse made a clean break with his past, but Boulby shows, to the contrary, how much continuity there really is in Hesse's writing and how much the themes and motifs of *Demian* are anticipated in Hesse's earlier works. The "break" is thus perhaps not as great as had been assumed. In pointing out elements of existentialism in *Demian*, Ziolkowski refers to Sartre, but Neumann shows how similar aspects of *Demian* are to the ideas of the German existentialist philosopher Karl Jaspers, for example the idea that Angst derives from the social isolation of persons like Sinclair and Demian who are "different" from the blindly conforming masses. Field, as the author of the latest book to appear on Hesse, is in a good position to give a balanced overview on most of the aspects of the novel highlighted by his critical predecessors.

To Hugo Ball and his 1927 biography of Hesse we are indebted for the personal details about Hesse's crises, including the sessions with Doctor Lang, which form the biographical background for the writing of *Demian*.

Almost all the critics stress the importance of Nietzschean thought to the philosophical background of the novel, and last not least Hesse's perennial preoccupation with the problem of the dichotomy between nature and spirit.

DEMIAN

ESSAY QUESTIONS AND ANSWERS

....

Question: Emil Sinclair is the hero of the novel, yet its title is *Demian*. Discuss.

Answer: It is true that the Bildungsroman is often named after its hero. Some famous examples which come to mind are Wieland's Agathon, Goethe's Wilhelm Meister, Novalis' Heinrich von Ofterdingen, and Keller's Green Henry.

Yet this is not always the case, as, for example, Jean Paul's Titan, Strifter's Indian Summer and Thomas Mann's The Magic Mountain indicate. It would seem that if the author does not use the protagonist's name as the title of his novel, then a title is usually chosen which in one way or another alludes either to the central theme of the novel or to an important feature of the hero's character. Seen in the light of this tradition, what does the title *Demian* mean?

It will be noted that the title is not Max Demian but simply *Demian*. The use of the full name would refer unequivocally to the individual person, whereas the simple surname is capable of being interpreted in a more impersonal and symbolic way.

The title, thus, does not refer so much to Sinclair's friend as an individual as it does to the principle he represents. Obviously, too, there would be little point in naming Emil Sinclair's story after someone else.

Since the novel is about Emil Sinclair's struggle to acquire for himself the characteristics his friend embodies (the novel ends, significantly, with the important statement that Sinclair's soul has come, at last, to resemble Demian's completely), then the title alludes at one and the same time to the central theme of the novel (the road to the realized Self-hood for which Max Demian stands) and to the most important aspect of Sinclair's character, namely the Demian-like self-realization he comes to achieve. The title thus functions as a type of cipher or code word alluding to the whole complex of motifs dealing with self-realization through which the novel's central theme is expressed.

Another reason for the title is the fact that the novel is supposed to be Emil Sinclair's autobiography. He does not immodestly name his story after himself. Rather, he looks to the guiding principle or decisive influence in his life for the title, and this brings him directly to *Demian*. Furthermore, if Hesse had named the novel Emil Sinclair or Sinclair he would in effect have made his hero refer to himself in the third person - a situation not befitting the first-person narrative of the story.

Finally, there is no doubt a purely practical reason for the title. To be perfectly frank about it, the unusual name Demian simply sounds more mysterious and interesting than does the more well-known Sinclair. An author must, after all, pick a title that sounds alluring, and Demian, with its fascinating suggestions of daimon and demon, fits the bill perfectly.

Question: Compare and contrast the roles of Max Demian and Frau Eva respectively in Emil Sinclair's life.

Answer: There is no conflict between Demian and Frau Eva. They do not compete for Sinclair's attention, nor does Sinclair feel in any way torn between the two. He realizes their essential identity, he sees in both of them that realized Self-hood based on totality or the synthesis of opposites which he is striving to attain. Their unity is expressed in the fact that they are mother and son, and also at the end of the novel when Demian gives Sinclair Frau Eva's kiss. It is Frau Eva's blessing but it is imparted by Demian. And yet there are some differences. Sinclair's soul comes to resemble Demian's completely at the end of the novel, but this identity is accomplished by internalizing the projections of Frau Eva, not Demian. It is the ashes of her painting he eats, not Demian's portrait. It is Frau Eva, not Demian, who is the means whereby the peaceful synthesis of the warring opposites in Sinclair's soul is effected, for only she is uniquely able to function as the common object both of Sinclair's spiritual devotion and physical desire, and this simultaneously, whereby the "light" and the "dark" sides of Sinclair's nature are brought together.

Question: What is the significance of the following statement of Emil Sinclair's: "There would be beautiful, tender and lovely things to tell about my childhood.... But I am only interested in the steps which I took in my life in order to get to myself.... Therefore, I will speak...only of those new things which happened to me, of those things which drove me on, which tore me loose."

Answer: This quotation could serve as a classic statement on the theme and style of the Bildungsroman. The theme of this genre is the inner development of the hero ("...the steps which I took in order to get to myself..."). Stylistically, the Bildungsroman, unlike the Western European and Russian social novel, does not present a smoothly flowing, tightly woven plot but focuses only episodically on those experiences of the hero which are relevant to his development ("...those things which drove me on, which tore me loose").

Question: Discuss the Knauer episode and its significance for the novel as a whole.

Answer: The Knauer episode occurs in chapter six, "Jacob's Struggle." It has to do with a disturbed boy, a fellow classmate of Sinclair's, who is going through a spiritual crisis due to the fact that he cannot accept his sexuality. Considering it base and filthy, he attempts to deny it completely and live solely in a "pure" and "spiritual" realm. Every time he fails in this impossible task he sinks deeper into paroxysms of self-hatred that culminate in a suicide attempt (from which Sinclair saves him). Knauer has noticed Sinclair and is attracted by that different air about him that Demian calls the mark of Cain. Surely, Knauer feels, Sinclair must possess the secret of chastity, perhaps in the form of some special cult or occult knowledge, but Sinclair tells him that each person must find his own answers to the problems of his life, that there are no tailor-made panaceas.

The Knauer episode repeats some of the major notes of the novel in a minor key, only here the role that Demian plays vis-a-vis Sinclair, Sinclair himself now assumes towards Knauer. Knauer is caught up in the same dualistic world out of which Sinclair is now emerging in chapter six. Knauer's efforts to suppress one half of his nature is misguided, of course, but a mere telling him that he is on the wrong path will not suffice (although Sinclair does do that). He has to find his own way on his own terms. We do not know what becomes of Knauer. Perhaps he will fight his way clear like Sinclair does, perhaps not. Before they part, however, Sinclair gives him a hint as to the direction in which the way to Self-hood lies: "We create gods and struggle with them and they bless us." What Sinclair is alluding to here is the process of projection and re-internalization of unconscious images which will undergo on his road to totality. And as a matter of fact, it is immediately after the encounter with Knauer that Sinclair is able, for the first time, after many false starts and unsuccessful attempts, to paint the all-important picture of Frau Eva.

Question: Some critics say that Emil Sinclair dies at the end of the novel. Can this view be maintained?

Answer: At the end of the novel Sinclair is lying severely wounded in an army hospital. Demian, also wounded and lying on the next bed, dies after giving Sinclair Frau Eva's kiss. What better end to the novel could there be than for Sinclair, its hero, to die, too, on the last page, in true romantic fashion? It is tempting to see the ending in this way, yet to do so would be false. Why is this?

The first and easiest answer is that Sinclair's death is impossible. He is, after all, the "author" of the novel. He cannot write it if he is dead. Nor can we assume that he somehow wrote or dictated the story while lying in the hospital. The novel is simply too long and involved to be a deathbed narrative. To make the fiction that Sinclair wrote the novel possible, he must have recovered. It should be remembered, too, that when Hesse published the novel pseudonymously in 1919 he wanted people to believe that there was a real Emil Sinclair alive in Switzerland.

But these are not the really important reasons. Sinclair must live because he is a representative of that new humanity in which lies the hope of the human race. Possessed now of self-realization and Frau Eva's blessing, it would make no sense for Hesse to bring him all this way only to have him die at the very moment when he is finally prepared to go out into the world and proclaim, Zarathustra-like, what Ziolkowski (*The Novels of Hermann Hesse*) calls "The Gospel of *Demian*."

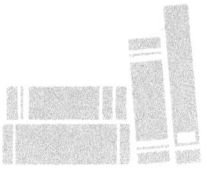

DEMIAN

BIBLIOGRAPHY

EDITIONS OF DEMIAN IN ENGLISH TRANSLATION

Demian, with foreword by Thomas Mann. New York: Holt, 1949. Hardcover. *Demian*. New York: Harper and Row, 1965. Hardcover. *Demian*. London: Vision Press, 1965. Hardcover. *Demian*. London: Panther Books, 1969. Paperback. *Demian*. New York: Bantam Books, 1971. Paperback.

Bibliographies On Hesse

Bareiss, Otto. *Hermann Hesse. Eine Bibliographie der Werke uber Hermann Hesse.* Basel: Karl Maier-Bader, vol. I, 1962; vol. II, 1964.

Mileck, Joseph. *Hermann Hesse and his Critics.* Chapel Hill: University of North Carolina Press, 1958. In three parts, only part three of which is a bibliography. Part one is "A Bio-Bibliographical Sketch" on "Hesse and his Art," and "Hesse and his Age." Part two is a detailed critical discussion and survey of the literature on Hesse. A valuable tool to the serious student.

Waibler, Helmut. *Hermann Hesse. Eine Bibliographie.* Berne, Munich: Francke, 1962. Most complete bibliography.

Books On Hesse

Ball, Hugo. *Hermann Hesse. Sein Leben und sein Werk.* New ed. cont. by Anni Carlsson and Otto Basler. Zurich: Fretz and Wasmuth, 1947. An uncritical but intimate biography up to 1927 by Hesse's friend. Later updated by Carlsson and Basler. Still the best biography.

Boulby, Mark. *Hermann Hesse. His Mind and Art.* Ithaca: Cornell U. P., 1967. An excellent in-depth study of the major prose.

Field, George W. *Hermann Hesse.* New York [*Twayne's World Authors*, no. 93], 1970. An excellent introductory study.

Rose, Ernest. *Faith from the Abyss. Hermann Hesse's Way from Romanticism to Modernity.* New York: Columbia, 1965. Studies Hesse's creative reaction to the German literary heritage.

Ziolkowski, Theodore. *The Novels of Hermann Hesse. A Study in Theme and Structure.* Princeton: Princeton U. P., 1965. An excellent in-breadth study of the major novels.

Ziolkowski, Theodore. *Hermann Hesse.* New York [*Columbia Essays on Modern Writers*, no. 22], 1966. The best thumbnail sketch of Hesse and his work.

Articles And Chapters On Hesse

Benn, Maurice. "An Interpretation of the Work of Herman Hesse." *German Life and Letters*, III (1949-50), 202-211. Excellent general discussion of Hesse's main works, stressing the Nature-Spirit dichotomy.

Boeckmann, Paul. "Hermann Hesse," in *Deutsche Literatur im 20. Jahrhundert.* Heidelberg: Rothe, 1954, 288-304. An excellent general discussion of Hesse and his place in German literature.

Brummer, John W. "The Natur-Geist Polarity in Hermann Hesse," in *Helen Adolf Festschrift*, ed. Sheema Z. Buehne. New York: F. Ungar, 268-284. The dichotomy of nature and spirit as a recurrent motif in Hesse.

Colby, Thomas E. "The Impertinent Prodigal: Hermann Hesse's Hero." *The German Quarterly*, XL (1967), 14-23. Sees Hesse's major **protagonists** as Prodigal Sons who, however, do not return to the Father (i.e. traditional authority).

Engel, Eva J. "Herman Hesse," in *German Men of Letters*, vol. II, London: Wolff, 1963, 249-274. An introductory essay.

Frickert, Kurt J. "The development of the Outsider Concept in Hesse's Novels." *Monatshefte*, LII (1960), 171-178. The conflict between the individual and society as exemplified in Hesse's heroes.

Koehler, Lotte. "Hermann Hesse," in *Deutsche Dichter der Moderne*, ed. Benno von Wiese. Berlin: E. Schmidt, 1965. An excellent general discussion of Hesse and his place in German literature.

Koester, Rudolf. "Self-Realization: Hesse's Reflections on Youth." *Monatshefte*, LVII (1965), 181-186. Hesse's treatment of youth as the time of vital struggle for identity.

Mileck, Joseph. "The Prose of Hermann Hesse: Life, Substance, Form." *The German Quarterly*, XXVII (1954), 163-174. Discusses Hesse's development as an author as going through three distinct phases reflecting Hesse's struggle with the meaning of life.

Naumann, Walter. "The Individual and Society in the Work of Hermann Hesse." *Monatshefte*, LIII (1961), 181-189. A perceptive discussion of one of the most important problems in Hesse's works.

Schwarz, Egon. "Herman Hesse, The American Youth Movement, and Problems of Literary Evaluation." *PMLA*, LXXXV (1970), 977-987. Discussion of reasons for Hesse's popularity among American youth.

Wilson, Colin. *The Outsider*. London: Gollancz, 1956. Contains sympathetic chapter on Hesse as a social rebel.

Ziolkowski, Theodore. "Saint Hesse among the Hippies." *American German Review*, XXV, 2 (Oct.-Aug., 1969), 18-23. Discussion of reasons for Hesse's popularity among American youth.

Articles And Chapters On Demian

NOTE: There are thoroughgoing discussions of *Demian* in chapters devoted to this novel in the books of Boulby, Field, Rose, and Ziolkowski, cited above. For further study of *Demian*, see:

Dahrendorf, Malte. "Hermann Hesse's *Demian* und C. G. Jung." *Germanisch-Romanische Monatsschrift*, XXXIX (1958). 81-97. The influence of Jungian psychology on *Demian*.

Matzig, Richard B. "*Demian*. Geburt eines Mythos" in *Hermann Hesse in Montagnola*. Basel: Amerbach, 1947, 15-30. Discussion of the mythopoetic background to *Demian*.

Mileck, Joseph. "Names and the Creative Process." *Monatshefte*, LIII (1961), 167-180. Discussion of the symbolic significance of the names of the major characters in *Demian* and other novels of Hesse.

Neumann, Erwin. "Hermann Hesses Roman *Demian* (1917). Eine Analyse." *Wissenschaftliche Zeitschrift der Padagogischen Hochschule Potsdam*, XII (1968), 673-695. A Marxist interpretation of *Demian*.

Seidlin, Oskar. "Herman Hesse. The Exorcism of the Demon." *Symposium*, IV (1950), 325-348. Argues against the psychoanalytical approach to *Demian* in favor of a spiritual and existential interpretation.

www.ingramcontent.com/pod-product-compliance
Lightning Source LLC
LaVergne TN
LVHW011727060526
838200LV00051B/3054